GCSE AQA English
Producing Non-Fiction Texts and Creative Writing
The Study Guide

This book is for anyone doing **GCSE AQA English** or **English Language** at foundation level.

It's a **step-by-step guide** to becoming an expert on the Producing Non-Fiction Texts section of your Unit 1 exam, and the Unit 3 Part b Creative Writing controlled assessment.

It's got **everything you need** — writing techniques, sample questions and worked answers — to help you get **the grade you want**.

It's ideal for use as a classroom study book or a revision guide.

What CGP is all about

Our sole aim here at CGP is to produce the highest quality books — carefully written, immaculately presented and dangerously close to being funny.

Then we work our socks off to get them out to you — at the cheapest possible prices.

CONTENTS

Section Six — The Exam

Section Seven — Creative Writing

Section Eight — The Controlled Assessment — English Language

Section Nine — The Controlled Assessment — English

Published by CGP

Editors:
Claire Boulter
Polly Cotterill
Katherine Craig
Edmund Robinson
Caley Simpson
Sarah Williams

Produced with:
Peter Thomas
Alison Smith
Nicola Woodfin

Contributors:
Caroline Bagshaw
Holly Bennett
Samantha Bensted
Fiona Ingram
Peter Inson
Ian Miles
Wendy Novak
Elisabeth Sanderson
Nicola Woodfin

With thanks to Rachael Powers and Carl Dowling for the proofreading.

ISBN: 978 1 84146 945 4
Groovy website: www.cgpbooks.co.uk

Jolly bits of clipart from CorelDRAW®
Printed by Elanders Ltd, Newcastle upon Tyne.

Based on the classic CGP style created by Richard Parsons.

How to Use this Book

This book will help you with the writing questions of your GCSE English/English Language exam. The writing questions are in section B of the Unit 1 exam. There's one question on 'informative or descriptive writing', and one question where you write to 'argue or persuade'. The last few sections will help you with the Unit 3 controlled assessment, where you have to do some creative writing.

The Assessment Objectives tell you what Skills you need

The assessment objectives are the things that AQA says you need to be able to do to get good marks for these bits of the GCSE. Don't worry — there aren't very many of them. Put simply, you have to:

1) Write clearly and imaginatively, using the appropriate language and form for your audience.

2) Organise your ideas into sentences, paragraphs and whole pieces of text, using a range of writing techniques and structures. This will make sure your ideas are well linked and easy to understand.

3) Use a variety of sentence structures, and use good punctuation and spelling.

Each Section of the book deals with a Different Skill

SECTION 1 is about the purpose (why you're writing), the audience (who you're writing for) and the form (whether you're writing a letter, article or advert etc).

SECTION 2 is about how to write to inform and explain.

SECTION 3 is about writing to describe.

Sections 1-7 are for both the English and English Language GCSEs.

SECTION 4 tells you how to write to argue and persuade.

SECTION 5 tells you how to write to advise.

SECTION 6 contains some example "producing non-fiction texts" questions — these will come up in the writing part of the Unit 1 exam. It also shows you the mark scheme for the exam, and some sample answers, working from a E grade up to a C.

SECTION 7 is about creative writing.

SECTION 8 tells you about the Controlled Assessment you have to do if you're doing GCSE English Language, and gives you some sample answers (from an E grade up to a C).

SECTION 9 tells you about the Controlled Assessment you have to do if you're doing GCSE English, and gives you some sample answers (from an E grade up to a C).

At the end of the book there's a handy glossary that gives you definitions of loads of important words and terms that you might need.

The book also doubles up as a rabbit hutch liner...

This book is full of straightforward ways of getting extra marks. Read through the explanations and examples and practise all the tips individually. Then try to include as many as you can in your work.

The Purpose of the Text

The writing exam questions will always tell you the <u>purpose</u> of the text you have to write — <u>why</u> the text is being written.

The Purpose is given in the Question

1) The <u>question</u> will tell you the <u>reason</u> you're writing the text. For example:

> Choose a time when you felt very angry and explain why you felt that way.

Here's the purpose.

'Text' just means a piece of writing.

2) Think about the <u>purpose</u> of your writing when you start <u>planning</u> your answer — and make sure your finished answer sticks to the purpose <u>all</u> the way through.

Each Exam Question has a different Purpose

You have to answer <u>two</u> different questions in your exam.

1) The first writing task involves <u>informative</u> or <u>descriptive</u> writing, e.g.

> Write a letter to a friend explaining why you want to get a pet.

This question is fairly <u>short</u>, and will probably include <u>details</u> of <u>your own experiences</u>.

2) The second writing question wants you to <u>take a particular viewpoint</u>, e.g.

> Some people think that teenagers should be taught to look after their money at school. Write an article arguing for or against this idea.

This question is a bit <u>longer</u> — you need to keep up your <u>argument</u> all the way through.

Sometimes a question has More than one Purpose

There could be a question in the exam with <u>more than one</u> purpose, e.g.

> Write a letter to a local business arguing that schools need more support and persuading them to help.

This question wants you to argue <u>and</u> persuade. Make sure you cover <u>both</u> purposes in your answer.

Every question has at least one porpoise.

Every essay has a purpose...

In this book, you'll learn how to write well for each purpose. The book's bursting with tips and information for improving your writing skills. So what are you waiting for? Get on with it!

The Purpose of the Text

Your writing must <u>suit the purpose</u> to get decent grades. It might seem like a lot of effort, but it's really worth it. Here are some important areas to work on.

Structure your writing to suit the Purpose

1) The <u>structure</u> of a piece of writing means how it's <u>organised</u> — which bits of the writing go where.

2) Work out the best <u>structure</u> for your answer before you start.

3) Use a structure that is suitable for your <u>purpose</u>. Writing to <u>inform</u> the council about a litter problem should have a different structure from writing to <u>persuade</u> businessmen to buy a car.

Here's an exam question:

> Write an article for your school paper in which you argue that teenagers are given a bad press.

Teenagers are often given a bad dress.

Here's one way you could <u>structure</u> the answer to this particular question:

1) Start by saying what the problem is in the introduction.

2) Then give some examples of unfair attitudes towards teenagers.

3) Go on to say why they're wrong.

4) Give some positive examples, e.g. teenagers helping in the community.

5) Finish by describing how you think things should change in the conclusion.

Choose your language Carefully

The purpose of your article for the school paper is to <u>argue</u> that teenagers are given a bad press. So you need to use language that will <u>convince</u> readers that you have a strong argument.

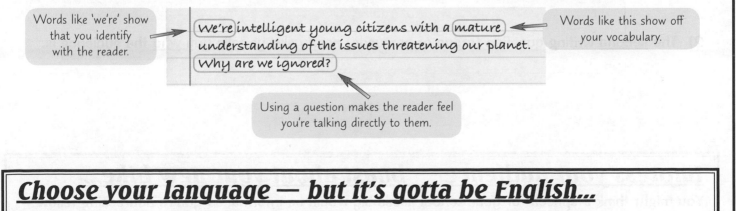

Words like 'we're' show that you identify with the reader.

We're intelligent young citizens with a mature understanding of the issues threatening our planet. Why are we ignored?

Words like this show off your vocabulary.

Using a question makes the reader feel you're talking directly to them.

Choose your language — but it's gotta be English...

Don't forget you're writing to show what you can do, so try to impress the examiner and you'll pick up lots of tasty marks. And remember that oily fish is good brain food.

The Audience

Sometimes the questions will tell you <u>who</u> you're writing for (the <u>audience</u>). Writing for teenagers is different from writing for your ancient and cantankerous head teacher. Oh yes.

Make sure your writing Style matches your Audience

Work out who your <u>audience</u> is <u>before</u> you start writing,
and think about what <u>style</u> you need to use:

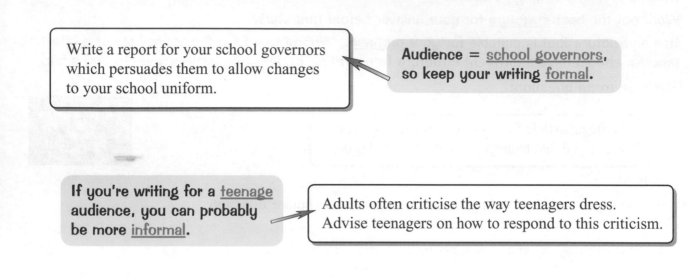

Write a report for your school governors which persuades them to allow changes to your school uniform.

Audience = <u>school governors</u>, so keep your writing <u>formal</u>.

If you're writing for a <u>teenage</u> audience, you can probably be more <u>informal</u>.

Adults often criticise the way teenagers dress. Advise teenagers on how to respond to this criticism.

Questions Don't always tell you Who the audience is

1) The <u>first</u> writing question (inform or describe) <u>might not</u> say who the writing is for.
    If that happens, just assume you're writing for the <u>examiner</u>.

If you could choose, where in the world would you like to live? Explain the reasons for your choice.

There's no obvious <u>audience</u>, so write your answer to the <u>examiner</u> here.

2) The <u>second</u> writing question (argue or persuade) nearly always <u>tells</u> you <u>who</u> the audience is.

Impress your audience — boast about your new bike...

You might think a speech for your school assembly would be informal as you're addressing fellow students, but think about it more carefully... If it's about a serious subject, then you might be better off making your speech more formal. There's more about all this on the next few pages.

The Audience

Matching your <u>writing style</u> to your <u>audience</u> is very important. Here are a few points to remember.

Don't make your Writing too Simple

1) If the question asks you to write to a <u>friend</u>, don't write too casually and <u>never</u> use <u>text talk</u>.

2) You can sound <u>chatty</u> but make sure you still include a <u>range</u> of sentences and vocabulary.

3) Being <u>sarcastic</u> or <u>humorous</u> can help you write 'to a friend' without writing too simply.

This is the sort of thing you <u>should</u> be writing:

> Of course I'm grateful that they allow me to slave tirelessly into the early hours of the morning.

Here are some examples of <u>what not to do</u>:

> His fiery, pungent, yet fragrant, aromatic odour reverberated resonantly in my vibrating nostrils.

This is a bit over the top and ridiculous.

> Mate, here's some goss 4 ya. That guy from skool u like stank like 2 much BO 2day.

No no no no. Absolutely not. Don't do this.

You may have to Write in Character

Sometimes you have to pretend to be an <u>expert</u> at something. Try to get in <u>character</u> a bit, but don't worry — you <u>won't</u> need lots of <u>specialist knowledge</u>.

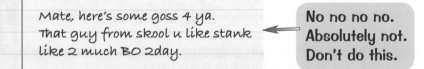

You've got to pretend to be a <u>successful celebrity</u>.

You are a (celebrity) who has won (awards) for your work. Write an article for (school leavers) advising them on how to succeed.

You can <u>choose</u> what you're famous for.

Use a <u>confident, encouraging</u> tone for this audience.

You're a brain surgeon — write an instruction manual...

The reason people sometimes come unstuck in English exams is because they weren't prepared. The earlier you learn all this stuff the easier you'll find it in the exam. You'll have time to get in plenty of practice in advance so it shouldn't be too scary when you're faced with the real thing.

Letters

You need to think about what <u>type</u> of text you're writing. Different types of text include letters, leaflets, magazine articles, speeches etc. This page is about writing a <u>letter</u>.

Some Letters need to be Formal

1) If the question asks you to write a <u>letter</u>, look at the <u>audience</u> to see if it needs to be formal. If it's to people you <u>don't know well</u>, or to people <u>in charge</u>, keep it <u>formal</u>, e.g.

> Write a letter to the head of a national charity, explaining how your school wants to help fundraise.

2) Start with a formal <u>greeting</u>, e.g. 'Dear Sir/Madam' or 'Dear Mrs Jones'.

3) <u>Sign off</u> formally too — 'Yours sincerely' if you've used their name, 'Yours faithfully' if you haven't.

4) Use <u>standard</u> English and <u>formal</u> vocabulary — don't get too chatty:

✗ So, Tony, hope you like our idea for fundraising. It'll be a right laugh.

Don't use language like this in a formal letter — it's too casual.

This is much better — lots of impressive formal language.

✓ In conclusion, Mr Tiptree, we hope that our ideas meet with your approval, and we look forward to participating in the first event in the near future.

If the letter hadn't started with "Yo guys!", they might have given Susan an interview.

Informal Letters are more Relaxed

If you're writing a letter to a <u>friend</u> or <u>relative</u>, or someone your own age, use a more <u>informal</u> tone.

1) Start with your reader's <u>name</u>. Sign off with 'best wishes' or 'see you soon'.

2) <u>Assume</u> the reader already knows certain things about you. Don't overdo it though — stick to the <u>main point</u> of the letter.

> I'm sure you'll remember how I feel about spiders. Well this was ten times worse.

Dear Mum, I've forgotten how to do exams...

When you're writing a letter, what you say and how you say it is more important than getting the layout right. You don't need to put addresses, dates or that sort of thing on your letter either.

Adverts, Leaflets and Articles

Adverts, leaflets and articles often come up in exam questions. Here are some of the basic rules about writing them. They don't let you draw things or colour in — the meanies.

Adverts have got to be Persuasive

1) If you're writing an advert, you need to persuade the reader that they want the thing being advertised.

2) The style of your advert should suit your audience and what you're advertising.

3) Use headings and subheadings (see p. 38) in your advert to grab the reader's attention.

Everybody loves cheese!

As seen on TV!

Four fun cheesy ideas
— with toast
— on biscuits
— in a cheesecake
— and many more!

High in
saturated fun*!
*and fat

Cheese. Better than having friends.
Sponsored by the cheese sellers of East Anglia.

> Write the text for a mobile phone advertisement which aims to persuade young men to buy the phone.

Leaflets are often Informative

> Write the text of a leaflet which informs tourists of what your area has to offer them.

1) If you have to write a leaflet, you can write in paragraphs, and include subheadings and bullet points.

2) You could be asked to write an informative leaflet, or one to explain or to advise.

3) Don't let your writing get too simple just because it's a leaflet. You still need to include some interesting language and a decent number of words.

Articles can have Different Audiences and Purposes

1) An article can be for a magazine or a newspaper.

2) Think about your audience — e.g. if you're writing for a school magazine, your audience will be other students.

3) If you're asked to write an article, look carefully at the purpose. You could be asked to argue, persuade, advise, inform or describe — or a combination of these.

If the purpose of the article was to turn children into dolls, it had obviously been successful.

Be creative, darling...

Whatever kind of text you're writing, you only have to write the words for it — you won't get any extra marks for colouring in your heading or drawing a picture. This should be obvious from the question anyway — the questions mostly say "write the text for" rather than "make a leaflet".

Other Types of Text

It's strange, but you might have to write a <u>spoken text</u> for a question in the exam. You might be asked to write the text for a speech or a radio broadcast, or something like that.

You might have to write Speeches or Radio Scripts

1) <u>Speech</u> and <u>radio script</u> questions often ask you to <u>argue</u> or <u>persuade</u>.

> Write the text for a speech in which you persuade local shopkeepers to get more involved in recycling activities.

This means that you can use plenty of <u>persuasive techniques</u> (see pages 30-33).

2) Imagine the words being spoken <u>aloud</u>:

> These accusations are hateful, hurtful and humiliating.

Alliteration (see p. 17) and using a set of three describing words make this statement sound strong and angry.

3) Even though the writing is going to be <u>spoken</u> out loud, you should still write in proper <u>sentences</u> with good <u>punctuation</u>.

Think about who your Audience is

1) If it's a speech, you can talk <u>directly</u> to your audience. Use 'I', 'you' and 'we' to keep the audience <u>involved</u>.

2) You could mention <u>why</u> everyone is there listening, e.g. "thanks for coming to show your support for this cause".

3) It's a good idea to show you <u>understand</u> your audience's point of view:

> You are probably sitting there wondering what gives me the right to tell you how to run your businesses.

You're guessing what they're thinking so you can deal with their worries.

Don't set out your writing like a Play Script

1) "<u>Write the text</u>" means don't worry about <u>fancy layout</u> — just write normally.

2) Make sure you write in clear <u>paragraphs</u>.

3) The examiner just wants to see if you can do the kind of writing that's <u>suitable</u> for this <u>audience</u> and <u>type</u> of writing.

Darren could always anticipate his audience's response — if only it was less hurtful.

But I wanted to write a gritty crime drama...

...that'll be screened at 2am on BBC4, with a hard-nosed copper who never does things by the book forced to partner an idealistic young recruit. As the two track down a sadistic serial killer they slowly create a bond, and when the killer... whaddya mean, it's not original?

Exam Technique

Before you start writing, it's a good idea to spend five minutes <u>planning</u> your <u>answer</u>. You don't actually get marks for your plan, but if you make one it'll help you write a <u>well-organised</u> and <u>thoughtful</u> answer. And that's where the good marks will come from.

Think about the Question...

<u>Underline</u> the key words in the question you've chosen.

This is the <u>type</u> of writing you need to do.

Here's your <u>audience</u>. You'll need to be quite formal if you're writing for teachers.

This is the <u>purpose</u> — you'll need to give plenty of good <u>reasons</u>.

> Write an <u>article</u> for a magazine for <u>teachers,</u> in which you <u>argue</u> that they should wear school uniform too.
> Remember to:
>   Write an article
>   Use language suitable for teachers
>   Argue your case

Read any bullet points too. They usually remind you about the <u>form</u>, <u>audience</u> and <u>purpose</u>.

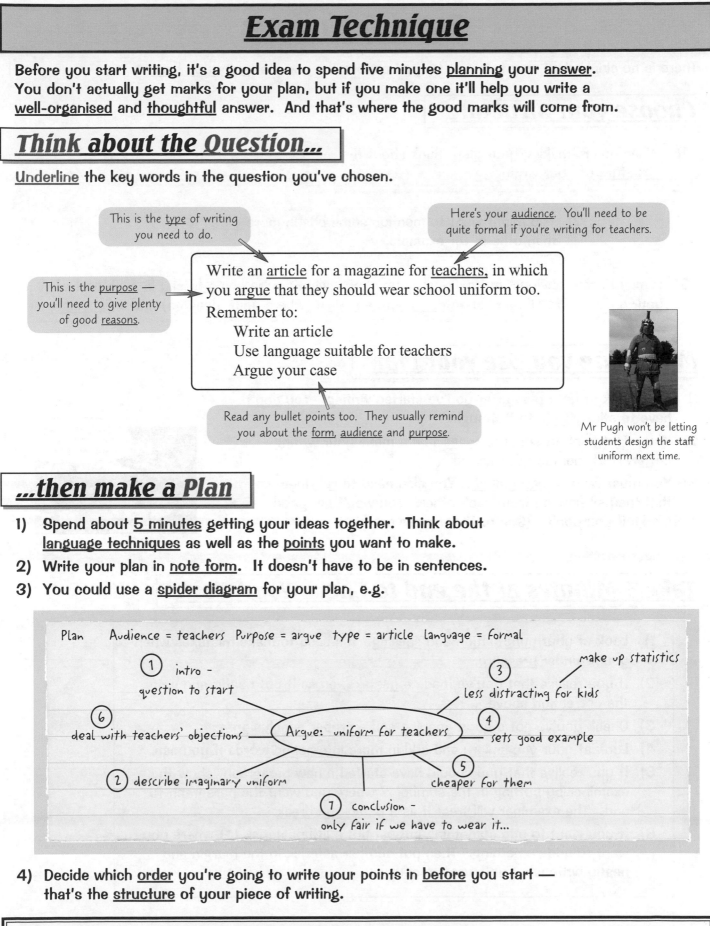

Mr Pugh won't be letting students design the staff uniform next time.

...then make a Plan

1) Spend about <u>5 minutes</u> getting your ideas together. Think about <u>language techniques</u> as well as the <u>points</u> you want to make.

2) Write your plan in <u>note form</u>. It doesn't have to be in sentences.

3) You could use a <u>spider diagram</u> for your plan, e.g.

Plan   Audience = teachers Purpose = argue type = article language = formal

① intro –
question to start

③ ——— make up statistics
less distracting for kids

⑥
deal with teachers' objections

Argue: uniform for teachers

④
sets good example

② describe imaginary uniform

⑤
cheaper for them

⑦ conclusion –
only fair if we have to wear it...

4) Decide which <u>order</u> you're going to write your points in <u>before</u> you start — that's the <u>structure</u> of your piece of writing.

Plan an escape route from the exam hall...

Now it's time for some planning practice. Try writing plans for some of the example exam questions we've printed in this section. Try using different types of plan, (invent your own method if you like) but don't spend more than 5 minutes on each one. There's more about planning on the next page and on p. 12.

Exam Technique

There is no single right way to plan. So just choose the one that <u>suits you best</u>.

Choose your Structure

1) While you're making your <u>plan</u>, think about the <u>structure</u> of your writing.

2) You might want to mention some bits in more <u>detail</u> than others, for example.

3) It might seem obvious, but make sure you know what you're <u>going to say</u> in each part of your answer. You'll need an <u>introduction</u>, a <u>middle</u> (where your ideas go) and a <u>conclusion</u>.

Make sure you Use your Plan

1) Look back at your plan <u>after</u> you've started writing. You <u>don't</u> have to stick <u>rigidly</u> to it though.

2) You might think of some <u>changes</u> that'd make your writing <u>better</u>. Put them in your answer.

3) You must write in <u>paragraphs</u>. You also need to <u>link</u> them so that they all flow on from each other. You won't get good marks if you don't. (See p. 17 for more on this.)

I tried to write it in paragraphs, but I can't find any in the stationery cupboard...

Take 5 Minutes at the end to Check Your Work

1) Look at your <u>punctuation</u> and <u>spelling</u>. It's easy to make mistakes when you're under <u>pressure</u>.

2) If you realise that you've made a <u>mistake</u>, <u>cross it out</u> neatly and write the <u>correction</u> above.

3) Check you've got a good <u>opening</u> and a proper <u>conclusion</u>.

4) Look at your <u>vocabulary</u> and add in more <u>interesting</u> words if you can.

5) If you realise that you should have started a new paragraph, <u>show</u> the examiner by putting in the symbol // where you want the paragraph to end. The examiner will treat it as a <u>paragraph break</u>.

6) If you want to <u>add</u> something in, just put a little <u>asterisk</u> (*) where you want to add something. Then put another asterisk in the margin and neatly write what you want to add.

Plans and structures — is this architecture or English?

Seriously though, don't panic when you see everyone else in the exam starting to write really fast straight away — they'll be writing rubbish. Take some time to read the questions carefully, pick the one you think you can answer best, then take 5 minutes to make a plan. It's the right way to do it.

Other Writing Tips

Here are some more ideas to help you prepare for the writing questions. They'll come in really handy when you're revising for the exam — no no, don't thank me — it's been a pleasure.

You Can Revise for English

There <u>are</u> things you can do before the exam which will <u>improve</u> your marks in the writing answers — it's <u>not</u> all natural talent, y'know.

1) Learn a list of words and phrases that help you <u>start sentences</u> in <u>different</u> ways. They're also useful for making <u>links</u> between paragraphs.

2) Practise writing in <u>paragraphs</u> and <u>linking</u> them together.

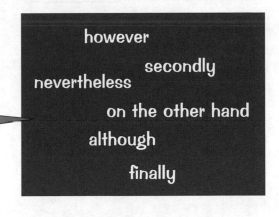

however

secondly

nevertheless

on the other hand

although

finally

Be Creative

1) Examiners want you to do <u>well</u>, and they're <u>looking out</u> for stuff to give you <u>marks</u> for. Have a go at things — don't be <u>shy</u> and think you'll look silly.

2) What you write doesn't have to be <u>true</u>. You can make things up or <u>exaggerate</u> and the examiner won't know or care, as long as you keep it realistic. They're only marking your <u>language skills</u>.

No, not that sort of creativity... tsk.

3) Use your <u>imagination</u> — don't just use really <u>obvious</u> words:

Blah blah blah. This is a pretty dull description.

There were some apple trees and the field was very muddy.

This is more interesting — there are some nice details and it gives you a much better idea of what it was really like.

Our feet sank into the soft clay soil as we walked, while the breeze brought the scent of the apple blossom from the neighbouring orchards.

Stimulate your brain — get a head massage...

You need to control your writing, especially vocabulary and sentence structure. It's better to write two sides of carefully chosen words than to ramble on for pages. And pages and pages and...

Planning Your Essay

Spider diagrams are a good way to jot down all your ideas and organise your thoughts.

Plan your ideas using a Spider Diagram

Remember, you'll write a better answer if you jot down your ideas at the start.

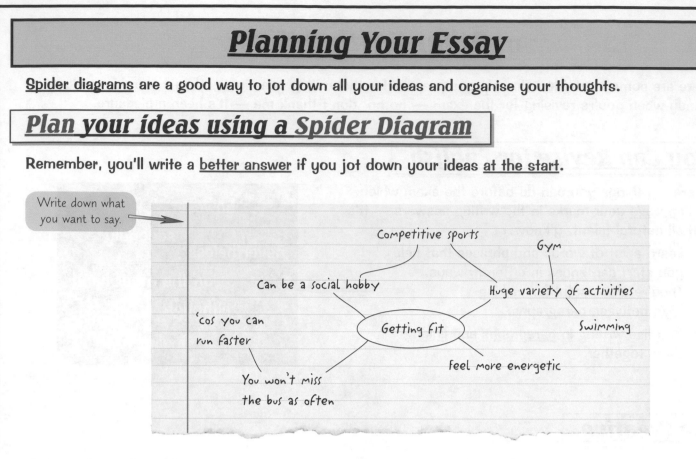

Write down what you want to say.

Competitive sports

Gym

Can be a social hobby

Huge variety of activities

'cos you can run faster

Getting fit

Swimming

You won't miss the bus as often

feel more energetic

Then work out the order you want to say your points in.

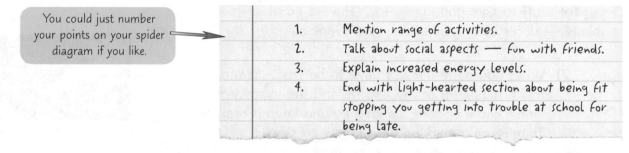

You could just number your points on your spider diagram if you like.

1. Mention range of activities.
2. Talk about social aspects — fun with friends.
3. Explain increased energy levels.
4. End with light-hearted section about being fit stopping you getting into trouble at school for being late.

Then all you need to do is write your answer... easy!

Organise the information Clearly

Think about the main things you want to say and note them down in a plan.
Here's an example of a "writing to inform" question.

Write an information leaflet about the sixth-form at your school for new students and their parents.

Purpose: to inform
Type of writing: leaflet
Audience: new students and their parents.
Points to include:
1) Sixth-form — 200 pupils.
2) There's loads of choice of AS-level subjects.
3) Students get good grades.

And here's a plan of the main points you could mention in your answer.

If you're scared of spiders do an octopus diagram instead...

Organising your ideas before you actually start writing your answer is a great idea.
It doesn't have to be really detailed — just outline the points you want your writing to include.

Spelling and Punctuation

You get separate marks for <u>spelling</u>, <u>punctuation</u> and the <u>structure</u> of your <u>sentences</u> in the writing sections — so make your work as accurate as possible. Don't avoid hard words just because you might spell them wrong, though.

Punctuation affects Meaning and Style

1) You must use <u>commas</u> and <u>full stops</u> to make your writing clear.
   Commas are particularly important when you're writing <u>long sentences</u>:

   > *Although it was raining, the pool, which reflected the moonlight at its edges, still preserved an unruffled surface.*

2) <u>Apostrophes</u> can be tricky. Learn the <u>two main uses</u> and you'll be fine:

   Put them where you've <u>missed out</u> letters: ⟹ | *It's a shame we didn't realise she'd be there.*

   Use them to show that something <u>belongs</u> to someone: ⟹ | *The cat's fear increased as the children's footsteps got closer and the boys' shouts were heard.*

   If a word like this is a <u>plural</u> and <u>already</u> ends in 's', just add an apostrophe <u>after</u> the 's'.

3) Check that you've put **!** and **?** where you need them,
   especially if you've written a <u>speech</u> or an <u>informal</u> piece.

Make your Spelling as Accurate as possible

1) You <u>don't</u> have to spell every single word right to get good marks — but try to show you can get <u>some</u> of the tricky ones right. Make your own <u>list</u> of words that you know you find difficult. Here are some tricky ones to get you started:

argument	conscience	favourite	immediately	conscious	necessarily
occasional	disappear	embarrassed	deceived	unnatural	

2) Learn the words in the box below. They are all words that <u>sound</u> the same but are spelt differently.

A werewherewear wolf

THERE and THEIR	They took <u>their</u> coats when they went <u>there</u>.
HERE and HEAR	I can't <u>hear</u> you from over <u>here</u>.
YOUR and YOU'RE	<u>You're</u> going to love <u>your</u> birthday present.
WE'RE, WHERE, WEAR and WERE	<u>We're</u> going to Malta, <u>where</u> we'll <u>wear</u> bikinis all day. We <u>were</u> going to go there last year, but we didn't.

The examiner also has to read your handwriting...

I'd love to, but I haven't room here to tell you how to spell every word you might ever need. Anyway, hopefully this page reminds you about the things you might need to learn before the exam.

Writing to Inform and Explain

When you write to <u>inform</u> you do what it says on the tin — you give people information.
It's the same for writing to <u>explain</u> — you have to explain something (pretty obvious really).

Writing to inform Tells the reader Facts

So what's writing to inform all about? Well...

1) Writing to inform means <u>telling</u> the reader about something in a <u>clear</u> way.

2) It can sometimes be <u>personal</u> and reveal stuff about the writer, e.g. an <u>important event</u> in their life. But it's mostly about <u>facts</u> not opinions.

There are Loads of different Types of Writing to Inform

Here are some <u>examples</u> of the sorts of thing you might have to write for an <u>informing</u> question:

> A <u>personal account</u> of a <u>school or club event</u>.

> A <u>letter</u> to your <u>head teacher</u> informing him or her about <u>plans</u> for the <u>school play</u>.

> It can be <u>formal</u> or <u>informal</u> — it depends on the <u>audience</u>.

> A <u>leaflet</u> about <u>things to do</u> in <u>your area</u>.

When writing to Explain, tell the audience Five Main Things

The best way to "write to explain" is to base your answer on five <u>key points</u>:

> The WHAT...   ...the HOW...   ...the WHERE...

> ...the WHEN...   ...and the WHY.

Wally wished he could explain to the audience why he was balancing a man on his nose.

In other words...
<u>What</u>'s going on, <u>how</u> it's happening, <u>where</u> and <u>when</u> it is, and <u>why</u> it's happening.

> An explanation of a personal experience or ambition.

for example... →

> Choose a time when you felt a very strong emotion and explain why you felt this way.

> An explanation of what might happen in the future.

for example... →

> Explain what life might be like in your home town in year 2050.

What? Why? How? Is this some sort of investigation...?

So, five words — what, how, where, when, why. I know they're only tiny words, but remember them 'cos they really are important. When it comes to your exam, you'll be glad that you took the time to learn these — you'll be putting together a great answer and that's what matters.

Audience

So, you know a bit about <u>writing to inform</u> and <u>explain</u> now, and here's a page telling you some more. This is the second step on the ladder to becoming an evil genius and taking over the world. Maybe.

Think about your Audience...

1) Explaining a hobby to a friend is <u>very different</u> from explaining a business proposal to a company.

2) So always think about <u>who</u> you're writing for.

3) Then you can <u>adapt</u> what you're writing to make it <u>suitable</u> and <u>interesting</u> for them.

...then Adapt what you Write

The <u>style</u> of this answer is quite <u>casual</u> to suit the <u>audience</u>.

> Write a letter to a friend explaining why you think that they would have enjoyed a holiday that you recently took.

> I've just arrived back from my break in Greece and I think it's a holiday that you would have really enjoyed too. There was a good variety of watersports to try, and I know that would really suit you.

An informal, chatty style.

If the question was for a <u>different</u> audience, you'd need to use a different <u>tone and style</u>.

For some texts you'll have to be more Formal

Here's a <u>good example</u> and a <u>bad example</u> of a leaflet about your <u>school</u>.

This is <u>good</u>:

> This is a first class sixth-form in an excellent school. 92% of students gain A-C at A-level.

Formal language that suits the audience of parents and new students.

This is <u>not</u> so good:

> We're much better than that crumbling wreck round the corner that calls itself a college.

Too informal for the audience.

Well my audience is you — and I'm writing to explain...

...about making your writing suitable for your audience. If you're writing to someone important, don't use slang or silliness. However, if you're writing to a friend, you can be a bit more chatty.

Structure

Once you know <u>what</u> you want to say, you need to think about <u>how</u> to say it — this is the most <u>important skill</u> when writing to inform or explain. It may not be a great party trick, but it's a start.

Start with an Introduction

When you're writing to inform, you should always <u>begin</u> with a <u>paragraph</u> that sets out the <u>main points</u> you want to tell your audience about.

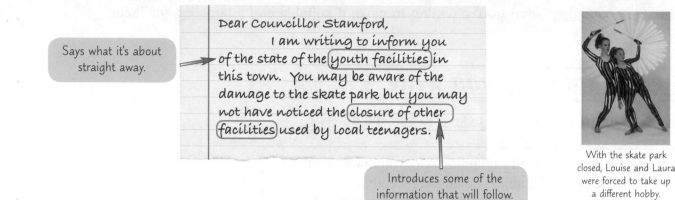

Says what it's about straight away.

Dear Councillor Stamford,
    I am writing to inform you of the state of the youth facilities in this town. You may be aware of the damage to the skate park but you may not have noticed the closure of other facilities used by local teenagers.

Introduces some of the information that will follow.

With the skate park closed, Louise and Laura were forced to take up a different hobby.

Your writing needs to be Clearly Organised

Use <u>headings</u>, <u>lists</u>, <u>bullet points</u> and <u>paragraphs</u> to make your writing <u>easy to follow</u>.

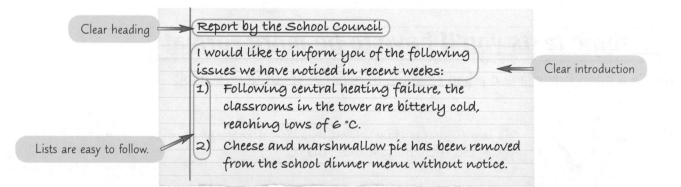

Clear heading

Report by the School Council

I would like to inform you of the following issues we have noticed in recent weeks:

Clear introduction

1) Following central heating failure, the classrooms in the tower are bitterly cold, reaching lows of 6 °C.

2) Cheese and marshmallow pie has been removed from the school dinner menu without notice.

Lists are easy to follow.

WARNING
Don't use too many lists or bullet points. The examiner needs to see that you can write in paragraphs with more detail too.

The governors decided it was cheaper to issue a new school uniform than to fix the central heating system.

Key is organisation to writing good — well, sort of...

Think about the organisation of your writing before you start. Otherwise the reader will get lost, you'll get no marks, the world will end and your mum will say "I told you so". Or something like that.

Structure

Once you've decided on the <u>points</u> you want to make, you need to think about how to <u>organise</u> them.

Link paragraphs together

<u>Organise</u> your ideas into <u>paragraphs</u>, and put them in a sensible <u>order</u>. If you <u>link your paragraphs together</u> you'll get more marks. Here are some useful phrases to <u>start</u> paragraphs with:

- Furthermore
- On the other hand
- In contrast
- However

Examiners love these phrases.

Subheadings *make your work easier to read*

1) An article can be split up using <u>subheadings</u> — these will help you <u>break up</u> your writing, attract the reader's <u>interest</u> and make the piece easier to remember.

2) Try to use <u>alliteration</u> (using several words that begin with the same letter) or <u>puns</u> (a play on words) in your subheadings to capture your reader's <u>attention</u>.

<u>Alliteration Attracts Attention</u>

<u>Fishermen Kept In Plaice</u>

Use a Clear Structure

1) When writing to explain, it's really important to <u>structure</u> your work clearly.

2) You need to <u>link</u> all your ideas together in a <u>sensible order</u>.

3) <u>Linking words</u> help you to do just that — they'll make your writing easy to follow.

Here are some linking words:

| firstly | secondly | then | furthermore | later |
| nevertheless | also | next | finally | afterwards |

Spot those linking words.

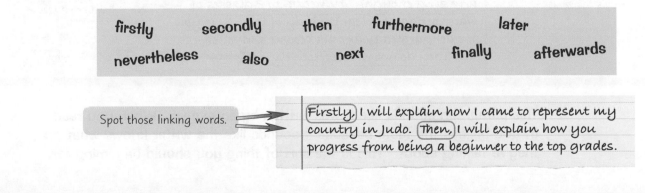

Firstly, I will explain how I came to represent my country in Judo. Then, I will explain how you progress from being a beginner to the top grades.

All clear and correct...

A clear structure makes your answer a lot easier to read. Furthermore, the examiners will love it and reward you with lots of nice juicy marks. Then you can go out and celebrate.

Techniques

A good way to sound convincing is to use <u>examples</u> and lots of <u>detail</u> in your writing.

You've got to sound Knowledgeable

It's a good idea to use <u>details</u>, <u>quotes</u> and <u>statistics</u> to back up your points. <u>Technical words</u> will also help you sound like you know what you're talking about.

The council transports 200 tonnes of recyclable glass from kerbside collections to the Materials Recycling Facility (MRF) every day.

Statistic used to add detail.

Technical words make it sound convincing.

The bears hoped their natty outfits would cover up their lack of flying experience.

Use Examples to Support your writing

1) Make sure you <u>back up</u> any points you make with an <u>example</u> or two.

2) Use <u>P.E.E.</u> (point, example, explanation) to <u>develop</u> your points (see p. 35). This will make your writing more <u>convincing</u>.

3) For example, imagine you're asked to explain what could be done about bullying in schools. As well as giving your ideas, you could <u>give examples</u> of what's being done at your school, and say whether or not it's making a difference.

Include lots of Details

1) A good explanation needs to include plenty of <u>detail</u>.

2) Remember to include the <u>who</u>, <u>what</u>, <u>how</u>, <u>where</u>, <u>when</u> and <u>why</u> in your explanation.

Here's the <u>who</u>.

A clear statement tells you what this paragraph will be about — it's the <u>what</u>.

Most people don't drink enough water. Are you drinking enough? You need 6 to 8 glasses of water per day to clear the body of toxins. If you are dehydrated your cells become shrivelled and they do not work effectively.

Here, some extra detail has been added.

This bit's the <u>why</u>.

This paragraph sounds like it was written by an <u>expert</u>. When you read it, you <u>believe</u> the facts because it sounds like the writer knows what they're talking about. This is the sort of thing you should be aiming for.

Recycling's not just for glass — it helps with English too...

Writing to inform and writing to explain both use loads of techniques from the other writing styles, e.g. they're often descriptive. So recycle the skills you learn elsewhere for these writing styles too.

Writing From Different Points of View

Think about <u>audience</u> and <u>purpose</u> when you're writing to explain or inform — it'll help you figure out if you should give a <u>balanced</u> or <u>one-sided</u> point of view.

You can write from a Neutral Viewpoint...

1) Writing from a <u>neutral viewpoint</u> means giving <u>all</u> the main points so that your writing isn't one-sided.

2) It's a <u>balanced</u> view rather than a one-sided personal opinion. For example:

> A study has shown that 80% of dog owners rated themselves as 'very happy', compared with only 30% of cat owners.

3) You should include plenty of <u>facts</u> and <u>statistics</u> so that your points sound more believable.

4) Try to sound <u>confident</u> so that your writing sounds like the <u>truth</u> rather than just an opinion.

For example, you'd write from a <u>neutral viewpoint</u> if you were writing to your MP <u>explaining</u> how facilities could be improved in your area:

Here are some statistics to back up the points.

> I am writing to you to explain how facilities could be improved in Madeuptown by giving more money to youth clubs. I help to run the local youth club and we have no money to buy things with. Madeuptown has lots of young people and more youth crime than other similar towns. Many residents of the town have said that providing these young people with something to do is important.

These sentences contain opinions, but it's OK — giving different opinions makes this more balanced.

...or use your own Opinions

1) In your exam, you could be asked to explain your <u>own view</u> on a topic.

2) This means you're giving your own <u>personal opinion</u>. In this sort of writing, it's OK to only mention what <u>you</u> think, and to give a <u>one-sided</u> account.
    Here's an example:

> I didn't know how much hard work was involved in nursing until I did my work experience. Shifts sometimes started at 5am! The uniform was a bit dull, but I wore it anyway.

Here's a personal opinion.

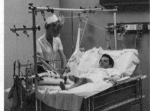

"The uniform may be dull," reflected Agatha. "But I have my boyfriend just where I want him."

I'd like a view of a Spanish beach...

I know it's tricky at first, but make sure you know the difference between writing from a neutral point of view and writing using your own opinion. Have a go at finding some examples around your home — e.g. look in newspapers and leaflets and then have a go at doing it yourself.

Writing Your Own

By now you should have the <u>theory</u> sorted, so it's time to put it all into <u>practice</u>.

Look out for these Examples of Writing to Inform or Explain

In your exam, you could get asked to write any of the following:

1) A Newspaper or Magazine Article

Write an article for a local newspaper, explaining an issue that is causing concern.

→ You're <u>informing</u> people about something that's happening.

Here's a possible introduction:

Mix of fact and opinion → Local residents are appealing against the council's decision to allow a music festival to go ahead in the town. Bands from all over Europe will arrive in Littleton and residents fear the huge crowds will cause problems.

2) An Account of an Event

Write an account informing the reader of a memorable event from your childhood.

→ This type of writing is more <u>personal</u>.

Here's an extract from an example answer:

Susie's passport photo...

My earliest memory is of going on holiday with my little sister, Susie. I remember being terrified of the planes — they were like giant birds swooping out of the sky.

Interesting detail

...never did improve.

3) A Letter

Write a letter to a local politician inviting them to attend a school debate. Explain all the necessary details.

→ This letter should be <u>formal</u> because it's to a politician.

Here's an extract from an example answer:

Formal, factual words → We would like to invite you to a debate about whether it is the government's responsibility to deal with childhood obesity. The debate will be held at 10.15am on Monday 22ⁿᵈ September.

Clear information

Letter to Father Christmas — formal or informal?

When you spot a writing to inform or explain question, the key to success is to work out who the audience is, what kind of document you need to write and what you need to give information about.

Writing Your Own

Here are some other types of exam question you might get. If you've <u>practised</u> all of these you'll be <u>prepared</u> for anything. Oh, except fire-eating of course — you'd better not try that just yet.

Don't forget these Types of Writing to Inform or Explain

4) A Leaflet

Write an information leaflet for a tourist attraction in your area.

The key to writing a good leaflet is to make sure it's well <u>organised</u>.

Here's an extract from a student's answer:

Use headings and subheadings

Use bullet points.

Things to see and do

Sampson's World of Steam is a great day out for all the family: Grandad will enjoy remembering the good old days of steam, and the kids will love the rides in our steam-powered funfair. Our exhibits include:
• A steam train dating from 1931 with trips around the park every 15 minutes.

Clear introduction

Give details

5) A Speech or a Talk

Write a talk explaining to new year seven pupils how best to settle into your school.

This talk needs <u>direct</u>, <u>informal</u>, <u>chatty language</u>.

Here's an extract from an answer:

Clear introductory paragraph

Friendly language

Good morning everyone and welcome to St. James's. My name is Timothy and I'm going to tell you a little bit about your new school. I've tried to make this talk useful, and not too boring.
Now, I know it all seems new and strange, but this is a friendly school and everyone will do their best to help you settle in.

Address your audience directly

Use these Phrases in your writing

Here are some really useful phrases for <u>writing to inform</u> or <u>explain</u>. Learn them before the exam.

I would like to inform you of...

Compare this with the...

One of the main points is...

It is important to...

Aaaaarrrggghhh — information overload...

When you're writing to inform or explain try to work out which pieces of information are important, and which should be left out to avoid overloading your audience. Plan ahead — it's the only way.

Writing to Describe

Descriptive writing is one of the things that crops up everywhere, so it's definitely worth knowing about.

You're painting a Picture with Words

1) When you're <u>writing to describe</u>, you need to remember that the <u>reader</u> won't have exactly the same <u>picture</u> in their head as you have in yours — you need to <u>draw it</u> for them with words.

2) You need to be as <u>creative</u> as you can, and come up with <u>inventive</u> ways to describe whatever it is you're thinking about.

Think about your Purpose and Audience

1) Your purpose is to <u>describe</u> — simple as that. You might be asked to "describe an object or place that means a lot to you" for example. So think about:

  - <u>what</u> it is that makes the object or place meaningful
  - <u>how</u> you can describe those things in detail

2) You might not be given a specific <u>audience</u> to write for, so just imagine you're writing for the person <u>marking</u> your work.

3) Try and base your answers on your <u>own experiences</u>.

Imagine you're making a Film of the scene

One good technique for describing a scene is to imagine that you're making a <u>film</u> of the scene, and that you're <u>describing</u> what you can <u>see</u>.

1) You could think about how the scene will <u>look</u> at <u>different times</u> of the day, or in <u>different seasons</u>.

> The beach was a desolate grey plain, empty of all life and movement apart from the soft splash of waves as they rearranged every pebble and stone. It was hard to believe that in less than a month the beach would be alive with tourists and deck chairs.

2) Or you could <u>zoom</u> in or out of your scene, <u>describing things</u> as you go.

> I was only feet away from the remaining fisherman, as he stood on the edge of the calm waters. Reflections shimmered on the surface, and in the distance I could just make out the shapes of hills.

Oh daarling, I'm simply overcome with all this loveliness...

OK, so all this "paint a picture with words" stuff might sound a bit airy fairy, but it really is the best way to get this right. Picture the scene in your mind and then tell the examiner about all the details.

Writing to Describe

You'll get extra marks if you can include <u>thoughts</u> and <u>feelings</u> when you're writing to describe.

Don't just state the Obvious

If you want to tell the reader how you <u>feel</u> about the thing you're describing, don't just write "I am frightened" or "I am happy" or whatever. It's much better if you use your descriptions to help the reader understand your <u>emotions</u>.

Imagine you're asked to "describe the room you are in". Rather than just giving the colours of the walls and describing the furniture, try to <u>show emotions</u> through your description, like this:

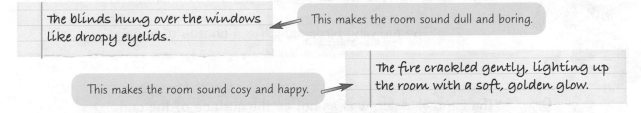

The blinds hung over the windows like droopy eyelids.

This makes the room sound dull and boring.

This makes the room sound cosy and happy.

The fire crackled gently, lighting up the room with a soft, golden glow.

Think about the Viewpoint you're going to write from

1) The <u>viewpoint</u> you write from can make your description more <u>interesting</u>.

2) If you're asked to write a description of a <u>zoo</u>, the way you describe it will be different depending on whether it's from <u>your viewpoint</u> or a <u>penguin's</u>:

- If you write as a visitor, you may want to create a sense of <u>fun</u> or <u>curiosity</u>.
- If you choose to write as a penguin, you could create a sense of <u>boredom</u> — another <u>forgettable</u> hour of being watched.

Use the Senses to improve your Description

Try and use the senses of <u>sound</u>, <u>sight</u> and <u>smell</u> in your description:

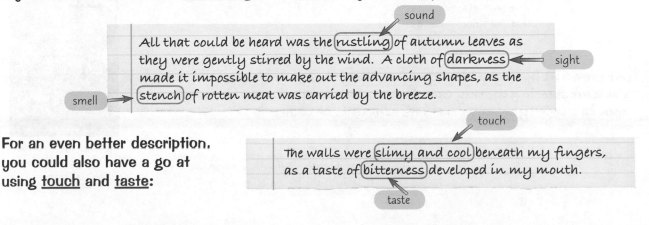

sound

All that could be heard was the rustling of autumn leaves as they were gently stirred by the wind. A cloth of darkness made it impossible to make out the advancing shapes, as the stench of rotten meat was carried by the breeze.

sight

smell

For an even better description, you could also have a go at using <u>touch</u> and <u>taste</u>:

touch

The walls were slimy and cool beneath my fingers, as a taste of bitterness developed in my mouth.

taste

Boredom? Rotten meat? Not in this book...

It really is worth taking a few extra seconds to come up with an unusual way of describing things — you can make fairly straightforward stuff sound much more interesting.

Imagery

Good writers often use <u>imagery</u> to create a <u>picture</u> in the reader's mind.
<u>Similes</u> and <u>metaphors</u> are types of imagery you might fancy using.

Use Imagery to develop your descriptions

<u>Similes</u> and <u>metaphors</u> are comparisons — they compare one thing to another.
They're really useful tools for <u>creating a picture</u> in the reader's mind.

<u>Similes</u> describe something by saying that it is <u>like</u> something else.
They usually use the words "<u>as</u>" or "<u>like</u>". For example:

"The morning birds sang <u>like</u> a chorus of angels."

<u>Or</u>:   "The lamb vindaloo was <u>as</u> hot as the surface of the sun."

<u>Metaphors</u> describe something by saying that it <u>is</u> something else.
For example:

"The night <u>is</u> a warm, damp blanket muffling the sound of traffic."

Use Imagery like this...

Using <u>imagery</u> in your writing really adds <u>expression</u> and makes the whole thing
much more <u>interesting</u>. Have a look at this description of an exam hall...

The sea metaphor shows
that the writer is nervous.

We are adrift in a sea of deep-blue floor tiles. The hands of the
clock are speeding up, they wait for me to look away and
then sail swiftly onwards. No safe harbour is in sight.

The sea metaphor from before is used again here.
It adds to the feeling of insecurity.

It turns out harbours
aren't great environments
for exams anyway.

This page is a glorious burst of golden sunshine...

Well OK, maybe not, but it's pretty important stuff so make sure you've got the hang of using
imagery, and that you know the difference between metaphors and similes.

Techniques

To keep your writing <u>interesting</u> (and to bag yourself some <u>big marks</u>), it's a good idea to vary the <u>length</u> and <u>structure</u> of your <u>sentences</u>. So read on...

Short Sentences <u>increase the Pace...</u>

To make description sound fast-moving and exciting, make your sentences <u>shorter</u>.
To make your description sound thoughtful and clever, make your sentences <u>longer</u>.

It's freezing out here.
Sandals were a bad choice.

SHORT: The sky darkened to leaden grey. Heavy rain hammered on the roof. The urge to scream was unbearable.

LONG: The last of the morning mist hung over the fields, a low lying cloud, swirling round my sandalled feet.

Use Compound <u>and Complex Sentences</u> like this...

If you can, use <u>compound</u> and <u>complex</u> sentences to keep your writing interesting and varied.
Here's how to turn simple sentences into compound or complex ones:

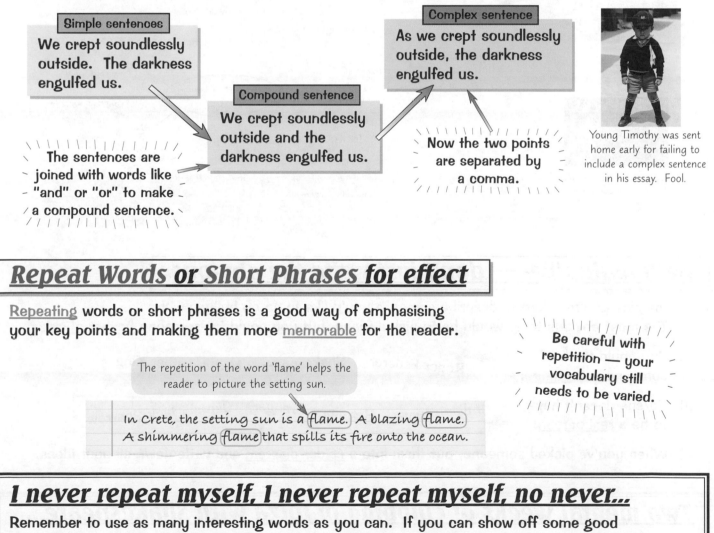

Simple sentences
We crept soundlessly outside. The darkness engulfed us.

Compound sentence
We crept soundlessly outside and the darkness engulfed us.

Complex sentence
As we crept soundlessly outside, the darkness engulfed us.

The sentences are joined with words like "and" or "or" to make a compound sentence.

Now the two points are separated by a comma.

Young Timothy was sent home early for failing to include a complex sentence in his essay. Fool.

Repeat Words <u>or Short Phrases</u> for effect

<u>Repeating</u> words or short phrases is a good way of emphasising your key points and making them more <u>memorable</u> for the reader.

Be careful with repetition — your vocabulary still needs to be varied.

The repetition of the word 'flame' helps the reader to picture the setting sun.

In Crete, the setting sun is a flame. A blazing flame. A shimmering flame that spills its fire onto the ocean.

I never repeat myself, I never repeat myself, no never...

Remember to use as many interesting words as you can. If you can show off some good vocabulary then the examiners will be thrilled. Well, fairly pleased. So instead of saying things like "walk quickly", you could use "scurry frantically", or "stride purposefully". Easy peasy...

Writing Your Own

Here are some more _practical tips_ on answering the question.

It's usually 'Describe a Place' or 'Describe a Person'

1) The "write to describe" questions usually ask you to talk about a _place_ or _person_.
2) You've got the chance to be really _imaginative_ and _creative_.
3) So it's a good idea to write all of your ideas down in a _plan_ before you set off.
4) If you were asked to describe a _terrifying place_, for example, you could get _ideas_ from anywhere:

> prison   war   first day at school   natural disasters   sci-fi films

Develop your ideas using Spider Diagrams

You could draw a _spider diagram_ as your plan to get some ideas flowing.

For a good description, think about _all five senses_. They're a great place to get ideas from.

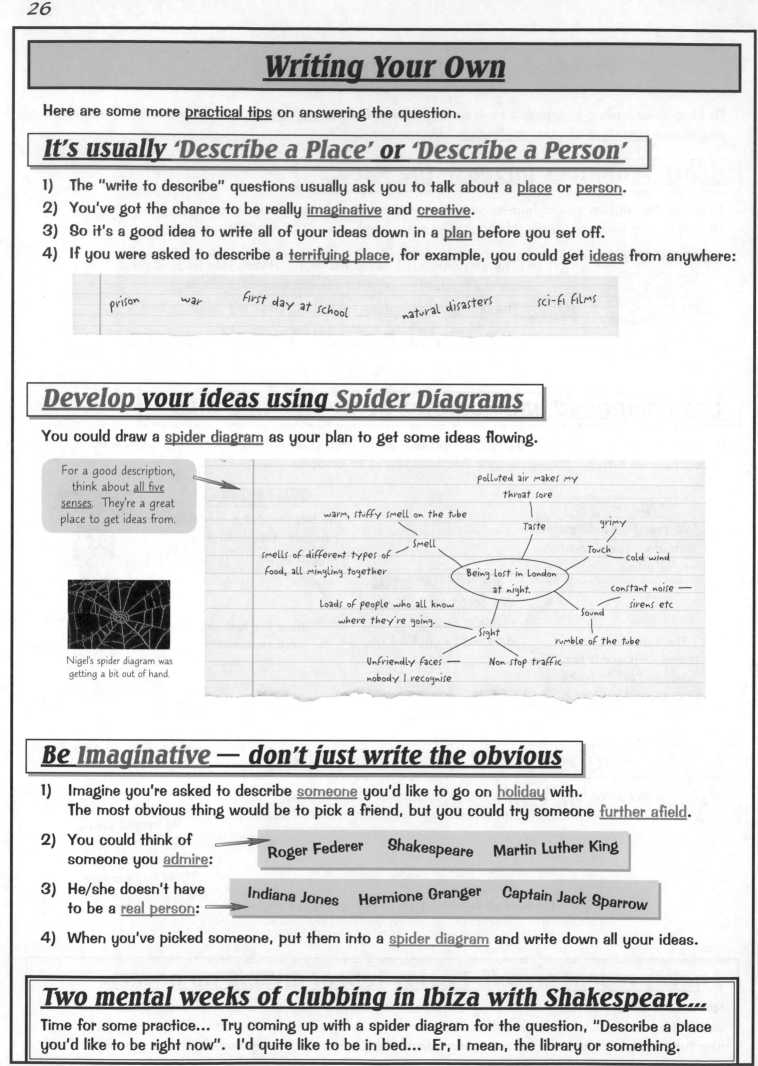

Nigel's spider diagram was getting a bit out of hand.

polluted air makes my throat sore

warm, stuffy smell on the tube

Taste   grimy

Smell   Touch — cold wind

smells of different types of food, all mingling together

Being lost in London at night.

constant noise —
sirens etc

Loads of people who all know where they're going.

Sound

Sight   rumble of the tube

Unfriendly faces — nobody I recognise   Non stop traffic

Be Imaginative — don't just write the obvious

1) Imagine you're asked to describe _someone_ you'd like to go on _holiday_ with. The most obvious thing would be to pick a friend, but you could try someone _further afield_.
2) You could think of someone you _admire_:

> Roger Federer   Shakespeare   Martin Luther King

3) He/she doesn't have to be a _real person_:

> Indiana Jones   Hermione Granger   Captain Jack Sparrow

4) When you've picked someone, put them into a _spider diagram_ and write down all your ideas.

Two mental weeks of clubbing in Ibiza with Shakespeare...

Time for some practice... Try coming up with a spider diagram for the question, "Describe a place you'd like to be right now". I'd quite like to be in bed... Er, I mean, the library or something.

Writing Your Own

Your writing needs three sections — a <u>start</u>, a well-structured <u>middle bit</u> and a <u>finish</u>.
You need to think about how best to keep the reader <u>interested</u> through all three parts.

Use your Introduction to grab the reader's Attention

Your <u>opening</u> has to <u>set the scene</u>, but more importantly, make your reader want to <u>read on</u>.

For example, for the '<u>terrifying place</u>' answer,
you could start with something <u>like this</u>:

> These words make the evening sound quite pleasant. They <u>contrast</u> with the mood later on.

> We stepped off the tube and (drifted carelessly) along the platform with the crowd. The crowd was a sea of faces I didn't recognise. We were spewed onto the street and a biting wind stung my face. I turned to take Jake's strong, warm hand in mine, but then, in a frantic panic (I realised he was nowhere to be seen.)

> It's clear that things aren't going well here — the reader will want to read on to find out what happens next.

In the Middle, try to keep things Interesting

You've got to keep the reader's attention throughout your writing — it's no good if they get bored halfway through. The middle of your essay is a good place to use some <u>imagery</u>.

It's so easy to get lost in London — there just aren't any landmarks to help you find the way.

> Every street I wandered down was a mirror image of the last one. Every street was a (lonely corridor.) No street would take me safely to the theatre I was trying to find.

> This metaphor emphasises how lonely and frightened the writer feels.

> The middle section is sometimes called the <u>development</u>.

At the End, you can go Back to the Start...

One idea for a good ending is to come back to the way you <u>started</u>.
Here's an ending to go with the story at the top of the page.

> When I finally found my way back to the station, Jake was standing waiting for me. He took my cold hand in his and we stepped into the warm comfort of the train.

ELEPHANT DUNG PYJAMAS — That got your attention...

Remember, you don't necessarily have to write a story. You'll get top marks for writing imaginatively, structuring your work carefully and using good vocab and stuff, whether it's fictional or not.

Writing to Argue and Persuade

Now you're going to learn how to <u>argue</u> and <u>persuade</u>. No, no, put your fists (and your money) away — it's not about fighting or bribery. It's about <u>putting across</u> your <u>point of view</u> successfully.

Here's what you'll get in the Exam

1) In section B of your Unit 1 exam, you have to answer <u>two questions</u>.
2) One of these questions will ask you to <u>argue</u>, <u>persuade</u> or <u>advise</u>.
3) Arguments can be written in different forms, e.g. <u>letters</u>, <u>reports</u>, <u>speeches</u> and <u>articles</u>.

Writing an argument Doesn't mean getting Angry

Writing to argue <u>doesn't</u> mean having a rant at the examiner.
What it <u>does</u> mean is putting across your <u>point of view</u> about a topic.

Persuasive writing tries to Change Opinions

Here are some types of persuasive writing that you could be asked to write in the exam:

1) A persuasive Letter

You could be asked to write a letter to a <u>newspaper</u> or to an <u>important person</u> like a politician to try to change their opinion about an issue. For example:

"Appalled" shows that the writer feels strongly about this.

I was appalled to find that, despite several complaints to the council, there are still no street lamps on Parkway Common. Something must be done urgently.

This persuades the reader to take action quickly.

2) A persuasive Speech

When you're writing a persuasive speech, think about how the words will <u>sound</u> when they're read out.

Repeating the 'u' sound here is an example of alliteration (see p. 17). It sounds effective read out loud.

Ladies and Gentlemen, we are here today to listen to the cases for and against the ugly, unfashionable and upsetting trend that is school uniform.

The speaker's opinions are obvious from the start.

Don't call the examiner a shrivelled up old toad either...

Writing for and against things is actually quite tricky. It's also hard to argue your point without name-calling and bursting into tears. Or maybe that's just me...

Writing to Argue and Persuade

The way you write to argue or persuade depends a lot on your <u>audience</u> — you'd use <u>different</u> <u>language</u> if you were writing for your <u>headteacher</u> than if you were writing for your <u>best friend</u>.

Think about the Purpose, Audience and Type of writing

1) You need to think about your <u>audience</u>, as this will affect the <u>style</u> of your writing.

2) If your audience is someone older and / or important then you need to use a <u>formal</u> style. If you're writing for other students, you can use a more <u>relaxed tone</u> and more <u>chatty language</u>.

3) When you get a question like this, the first thing to do is read it <u>carefully</u>. Here's an example:

> Write a letter to your headteacher arguing for or against young people being taught to drive at school.

4) Then jot down the <u>purpose</u>, <u>audience</u> and <u>type</u> of writing for the question.

5) For this question, the <u>purpose</u> is to <u>argue</u> and the <u>type</u> is a <u>letter</u>.

6) Your audience is your <u>headteacher</u>. This means you need to be quite <u>formal</u> and <u>serious</u>.

7) Also check whether you've been asked to argue <u>for</u> something, <u>against</u> something, or whether you can <u>decide</u> this for yourself. In the question above, you can decide for yourself.

Adverts try to persuade you to Buy Something

<u>Adverts</u> are really obvious examples of persuasive writing.
Their purpose is to try to persuade you to <u>buy</u> something.

> New Sparkly Brite washing powder leaves your whites 50% brighter than the leading brand. It's the freshest smelling too. Mmm.

This is only an opinion, but it's presented like a fact.

Facts and figures help back-up your claims.

There are other types of persuasive writing that you might have to write — think about <u>magazine</u> <u>articles</u> with a persuasive tone and persuasive <u>leaflets</u>.

I'd rather do GCSE driving than GCSE English...

There are many other types of persuasive writing that you could be asked to use — you might have to persuade <u>tourists</u> to visit your town or persuade <u>parents</u> that your school is great.

Structure and Techniques

Blimey there are a lot of techniques on these pages. They're all jolly useful though.

Use Language to get an emotional reaction

1) One way to persuade people is to encourage them to <u>react</u>, e.g. with fear, anger or sympathy.

2) Use <u>describing words</u> to make the reader feel <u>strong emotions</u>. For example:

Good describing words persuade the reader to see things your way.

→ These (cruel) scientists use (innocent, friendly and helpless) rabbits in their experiments. The unfortunate creatures might otherwise be loved by a child in a kind home. ←

These three words together build up a picture of the rabbit as a victim.

Compliments get you everywhere

1) If you <u>compliment</u> your readers, they'll think you have good taste and will be more likely to agree with you on your other points. Clever...

2) Tell them how much you <u>value</u> them or that you know how <u>clever</u> they are.

3) If you're writing an advert, say good things about the <u>product</u> or <u>idea</u> that you're trying to advertise. For example, include phrases that use the word "<u>most</u>" or words that have -<u>est</u> at the end, (e.g. "the fastest, most dazzling horse").

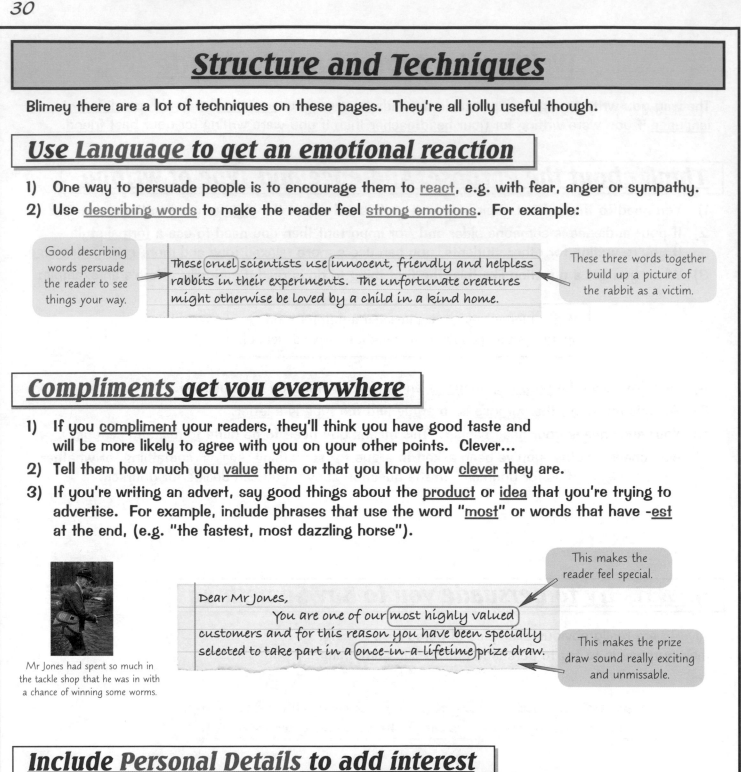

Mr Jones had spent so much in the tackle shop that he was in with a chance of winning some worms.

This makes the reader feel special.

Dear Mr Jones,
You are one of our (most highly valued) customers and for this reason you have been specially selected to take part in a (once-in-a-lifetime) prize draw.

This makes the prize draw sound really exciting and unmissable.

Include Personal Details to add interest

1) You can make your writing more persuasive by including <u>real-life examples</u> from your own experience.

2) Keep these <u>short</u> and make sure they <u>back-up</u> what you're saying.

I think that the service at the leisure centre is terrible, and improvements need to be made. When (I) first came to the leisure centre (I) was shocked to find that there was nowhere to get a free drink of water. (I) remember how thirsty (I) felt.

Using first-hand experience makes your argument appear stronger.

If compliments get you everywhere, why do we use cars?

If you're nice to people, they're more likely to listen to your point of view. So writing positively and giving a few compliments can be really persuasive. It's a clever trick to remember.

Structure and Techniques

If you really want to persuade people, back up your arguments with <u>examples</u>, <u>quotations</u> and <u>statistics</u> from suitable sources or experts.

Use Facts and Statistics to prove your point

1) Try to include some <u>facts</u> and <u>statistics</u> in your writing.
2) You can make these up if you like, but make sure they sound <u>realistic</u>.

This statistic sounds convincing, even if it's not really true.

> 70% of students agree that if they are wearing a school uniform, they are less likely to behave badly on their way to and from school.

Tony thought the fact that 100% of turkeys said they disagreed with Christmas ought to count for something.

Present Opinions as Facts

<u>Facts</u> are true. <u>Opinions</u> are what someone <u>believes</u> to be true, even if they're not. A great way to make your writing persuasive is by presenting your <u>opinions as facts</u>.

This makes it sound true even though it's an opinion.

> It is obvious that this is a brilliant school and it is clear that everyone who attends it will do very well.

This phrase also makes the opinion sound like a fact.

Quote Authorities to convince your audience

1) You can make your argument sound even more <u>convincing</u> if you <u>quote</u> people who would be expected to know about the subject.
2) You could quote doctors, scientists, politicians etc.
3) Again, you can make these up — just make sure they sound <u>believable</u>.

Quoting experts makes your argument sound better.

> Scientists at NASA have recently proved that the human body is not designed to stand still for more than 7 minutes at a time. Professor Hank Dupree said, "We've discovered that it's highly unnatural for humans to stand still for long periods". Yet during assembly we are frequently forced to stand for over 20 minutes.

Using quotation marks (" ") to quote someone directly can work really well.

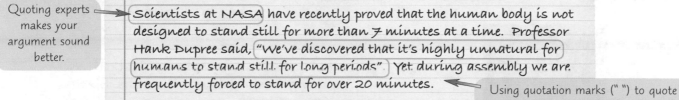

83% of students skipped right past this page...

You're allowed to make up facts, statistics and quotes. You don't even have to learn facts before you go into your exam — you can just make them up. Shame you can't do that with Geography.

Structure and Techniques

Righty-ho. On this page we have some of the most <u>incredible</u> stuff you'll ever learn in your life and we discuss why ants can't look left. OK, OK, I'm exaggerating — but it's just as interesting. Honest.

Exaggeration can give your ideas loads more Oomph

1) <u>Exaggeration</u> is when you make things sound much bigger/smaller or better/worse than they really are. E.g. "That was the most disgusting thing I've ever seen", when actually you've seen plenty of more disgusting things in the past.

2) Exaggeration makes your points seem more <u>important</u> to the reader.

3) This works well in persuasive writing. If there is a <u>problem</u> with something, say there is a <u>huge problem</u> with it. If you think something is <u>bad</u>, say you are <u>appalled and disgusted</u> by it.

Here's an example:

What a lovely exaggeration.

> Statistics show that in over 15% of cases, doctors have failed to diagnose the illness correctly. This is the most serious problem to face the NHS in recent years.

Questions can be really persuasive

1) Use questions in arguments to <u>make a point</u> rather than to ask for answers.

2) You can use them to <u>involve</u> the reader as it makes it seem as if you're <u>talking</u> directly to them.

> Would you let a child die of hunger?

Remember — a question that doesn't need an answer is called a rhetorical question.

> How would you like to earn cash in your free time?

> Surely it's time that students had more of a say in running this school?

Add Generalisations to sound more convincing

1) Generalisations are <u>sweeping statements</u> about a subject.

2) They're a good way to sound <u>forceful</u> and <u>convincing</u>.

3) Try using words like '<u>everyone</u>', '<u>all</u>', and '<u>always</u>'.

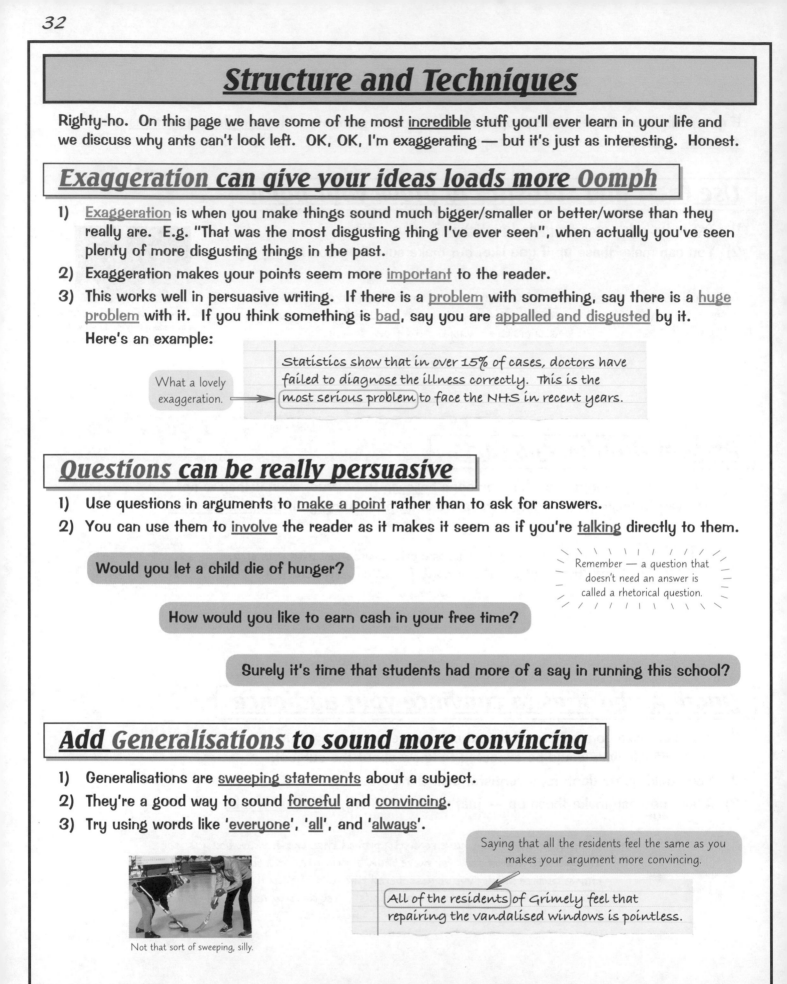

Not that sort of sweeping, silly.

Saying that all the residents feel the same as you makes your argument more convincing.

> All of the residents of Grimely feel that repairing the vandalised windows is pointless.

Ask me no questions and I'll tell you no lies...

It may be difficult to come up with a good one, but a well thought-out question can work really well if you put it in the right place. It gets people involved in the topic.

Structure and Techniques

Last page of techniques now. I know there are a lot, but they're all dead useful.

Include Opinions which are Different from yours

Writing to argue is all about giving opinions, but remember to include some opinions which go against your argument. You can then say why these other opinions are wrong — which will make your argument seem much stronger:

> You should include opinions which are different from yours...

70% of teachers claim that they wouldn't have enough time to cover the rest of the curriculum if driving lessons were introduced. However, by providing driving lessons after school or during lunch times, lesson time wouldn't be reduced.

> ...but then you can go on to explain why you think they're wrong.

Write about the Past, Present and Future

1) Writing about different times is a good way of building up the points in your argument.
2) Start in the past, move to the present and then you can even talk about the future if you fancy.

> This paragraph covers the past, present and future.

I used to believe that everyone had the right to own a dog. Now I believe that too many people buy them as status symbols and do not keep them under proper control. In future I think that people should have to pass a test before they are allowed to own a dog.

Repeat Things to emphasise key points

1) You can repeat words or short phrases to emphasise your key points.
2) In particular, repeating things three times is a clever trick that will help your reader to remember your points. This is called the "rule of three".

"...homework makes me travel sick when I copy it off my friend on the bus to school..."

It's unfair to suggest that pupils don't work hard. It's unfair to suggest that we are all lazy good-for-nothings. And it's especially unfair to expect us to take on even more homework.

> Three uses of "unfair" make the points stand out here.

'Talk to the hand' is not a good writing technique...

What a lot of techniques. I'm sure you got pretty exhausted reading about all those. I think it's time you took a break now and had a cup of tea and a nice chocolate biscuit. You deserve it.

Writing Your Own

OK, that covers writing techniques for arguing and persuading. Now it's time to do what matters — this page is about you (yes, you) answering an exam question.

Decide on your Argument

1) You need to decide whether you are going to argue for or against a topic, e.g. being taught to drive in school.

2) Once you have decided whether you are for or against, you need to jot down points which support your viewpoint.

3) Then decide which points to include and in which order.

health and safety issues
curriculum already too full
too expensive
AGAINST
not the job of a school
some pupils aren't mature or responsible enough
insurance costs

Think about your Audience

For example, you should be formal when you're writing to your head teacher:

Dear Mrs Hughes,
    I wish to express my concerns about our school's lack of healthy school lunch options.

Express yourself Clearly

Once you have written an introduction outlining your main point, you need to:

1) Build up the detail by writing down all the points which support your view.

2) Make sure you write every point clearly and fully in a separate paragraph.

Don't throw all your points at them at once.

Year after year, we have worn the same tasteless, dull and uncomfortable uniform. It is expensive to buy, £159 altogether, and gives our school a reputation for being old-fashioned.

Use evidence to back up your point.

Good list of three describing words here.

Remember to include an Introduction and Conclusion

Use the introduction to explain briefly what your argument is.

Dear Mr Delaney,
    Thank you for asking for students' views on the proposed removal of the snack machines from the school canteen. I believe that this is an excellent idea.

Use the conclusion to sum up your argument. This is a good place to try and get the reader to react emotionally.

Taking all of these points into consideration, I hope that you will change your minds and turn the leisure centre into a community resource which everyone can enjoy.

The fun way to tackle letters — trip up the postman...

Don't try this at home, kids. There are a few key things you've got to remember in the exam: Read the question, plan your answer, write in paragraphs and check your work at the end. Sorted.

Writing Your Own

There are a few more things to think about before you can set off and write your masterpiece of an argument. First you should think about paragraphs and P.E.E.

Use Paragraphs which Link together

Each point you make needs to be in a separate paragraph. The best way to fit the paragraphs together is to use a range of special phrases like these:

Beginning your argument:	Developing your argument:	Challenging other people's views:
It is clear that...	Another reason is...	Despite the view that...
There is evidence that...	Also...	Although some people say that...
Most people know that...	In addition...	However...
Research shows...	Firstly...	On the other hand...
	Secondly... (etc.)	

Use P.E.E. to develop your points

P.E.E. means making a Point, giving an Example and then Explaining how the example backs up your point. This will make your writing really clear. For example:

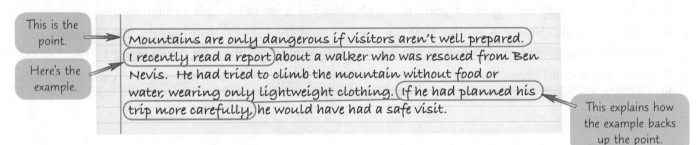

This is the point.

Here's the example.

Mountains are only dangerous if visitors aren't well prepared. I recently read a report about a walker who was rescued from Ben Nevis. He had tried to climb the mountain without food or water, wearing only lightweight clothing. If he had planned his trip more carefully, he would have had a safe visit.

This explains how the example backs up the point.

Include some of the Techniques of writing to argue

Don't forget to include some of the techniques covered on the previous pages. Here's an example which includes a few of the techniques:

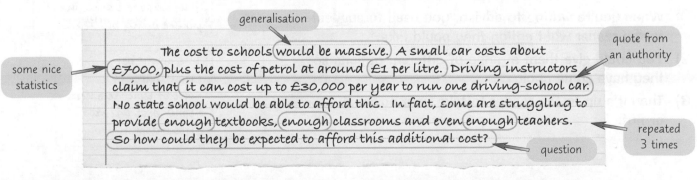

generalisation

quote from an authority

some nice statistics

The cost to schools would be massive. A small car costs about £7000, plus the cost of petrol at around £1 per litre. Driving instructors claim that it can cost up to £30,000 per year to run one driving-school car. No state school would be able to afford this. In fact, some are struggling to provide enough textbooks, enough classrooms and even enough teachers. So how could they be expected to afford this additional cost?

repeated 3 times

question

There is evidence that GCSE English isn't that bad...

OK, so you shouldn't have any trouble with this. Just decide what you're going to write, start with an introduction, use P.E.E., write in linked paragraphs and write a conclusion to finish. It will be OK.

Writing to Advise

Writing to advise is a bit weird — it's a mixture of informing and persuading. The main thing to remember when you're writing to advise is that you want to <u>help</u> the reader.

There are many different *Types* of advice

From 'how to quit smoking' leaflets to agony aunt pages, written advice is <u>everywhere</u>. Here are a few <u>examples</u> of the sorts of advice you could be asked to write in your exam:

- <u>Leaflets</u> e.g. how to find a good summer job
- <u>Magazine and newspaper articles</u> e.g. how to eat a healthy diet
- <u>Speeches</u> e.g. to advise new pupils about your school's rules
- <u>Magazine features</u> e.g. what to do if you're being bullied

Dear Jim, yes it is hard looking this smug all the time. My advice would be...

Written Advice *needs to be* Reassuring

1) Written advice has got to get the <u>reader's attention</u>. A good <u>heading</u> helps.

2) It's got to be <u>clear</u> what the advice is <u>about</u> so that people can decide whether to read it. A leaflet on healthy eating is no good if it <u>looks</u> like it's a leaflet on bike maintenance...

3) You also need to show the reader that you <u>understand</u> the <u>issue</u>. You can do this by using <u>technical language</u> and by sounding <u>confident</u>. The reader will then be more likely to <u>trust</u> you.

4) Finally, you should show that you understand their <u>feelings</u> and their <u>situation</u>. You can do this by using a <u>reassuring tone</u>. Here's a good example:

> Remember — you're not on your own. There are lots of people you can turn to who understand what it's like to be bullied.

Tell your reader what *Action* to take

1) When you're writing to advise, you need to suggest to the reader what <u>action</u> they could take.

2) You could give them a <u>range</u> of different <u>options</u> so they have some <u>choice</u>.

3) Then it's up to the <u>reader</u> to take your advice... or not.

> You must tell someone if you're being bullied.

> This could be:
> - your parents
> - one of your teachers
> - your best friend
> - your doctor

My parents call it advising... I call it nagging...

State what you're going to advise on, reassure the reader and then give them an action plan. With these three little steps you too can fulfil your life's ambition and become an agony aunt.

Writing Style

Writing to advise is a bit like archery — you need to know what (well, who) you're aiming at.
You're <u>more likely</u> to get your advice across if you write to your audience in the <u>right</u> way.

The writing style will depend on the Audience

1) You need to know <u>who</u> you're aiming your advice at. The <u>style</u> of language you use will depend on who your <u>audience</u> is.

   For example:

   > Write an advice leaflet for victims of school bullying.

   This is a bit too posh and formal if you're writing to young people.

   ✗ You should endeavour not to react to the bullies. It is far more effective if you ignore them.

   ✓ Try not to answer back or lash out at the bullies. It's better if you just ignore them.

   Change a few of the words you use to make the advice much more informal and friendly.

   Ben soon realised that lashing out at bulls is never a very good idea.

2) If you use the right style, your writing will be more <u>useful</u> to the reader, and they'll <u>pay attention</u> to your <u>advice</u>.

3) Writing style also depends on the <u>topic</u> — if it's a very serious topic you'll probably need to write more <u>formally</u>.

Tell the reader their Options

When writing to advise, you need to <u>tell</u> the reader what <u>options</u> they've got (using words like '<u>could</u>'), as well as saying what you think they <u>should</u> do. Here's an example:

> You could revise with friends, use a revision website, or do lots of practice questions. Whatever you do, you should put in at least an hour's revision a day.

I could love exams... and pigs might fly...

Texts that advise usually sound more friendly and less "in-your-face" than texts that argue or persuade. People usually read them because they want to know about something.

Structure and Techniques

Here's some handy stuff to help you when you're <u>writing to advise</u>.

Use Headings and Bullet Points

Use <u>headings</u>, <u>subheadings</u> and <u>bullet points</u> to <u>separate</u> different points of advice. Make sure you still have some <u>proper paragraphs</u> though — don't split your writing into too many short sections.

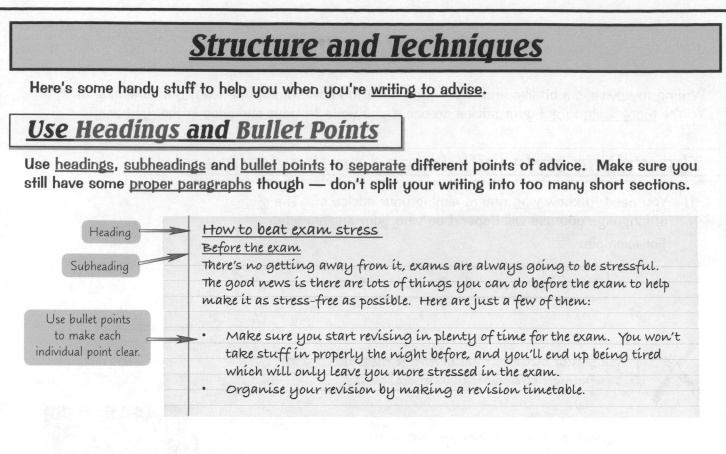

Heading

Subheading

Use bullet points to make each individual point clear.

How to beat exam stress

Before the exam
There's no getting away from it, exams are always going to be stressful. The good news is there are lots of things you can do before the exam to help make it as stress-free as possible. Here are just a few of them:

- Make sure you start revising in plenty of time for the exam. You won't take stuff in properly the night before, and you'll end up being tired which will only leave you more stressed in the exam.
- Organise your revision by making a revision timetable.

Ask Questions and give Answers

Here's another way to structure your advice:

1) Think about what <u>questions</u> your reader might have and use them as <u>subheadings</u>.

2) Go on to <u>answer</u> these questions <u>directly</u> in each section.

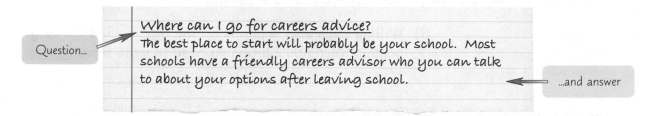

Question...

Where can I go for careers advice?
The best place to start will probably be your school. Most schools have a friendly careers advisor who you can talk to about your options after leaving school.

...and answer

Say How, When, What, Where and Why

When you're writing to advise remember to say <u>how</u>, <u>when</u>, <u>what</u>, <u>where</u> and <u>why</u> about the advice you're giving.

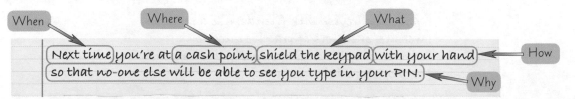

When

Where

What

Next time you're at a cash point, shield the keypad with your hand so that no-one else will be able to see you type in your PIN.

How

Why

If you have a question, put your hand up...

It's a bit like teaching a dog to do tricks.... sit, stay, heel, roll over, shake hands... Although I'm sure you won't be advising too many people to give you their paw for a doggy biscuit in your exam.

Writing Your Own

Plans are really important. Ask any evil genius or criminal mastermind, and I bet they'd tell you they wouldn't be where they are today if they hadn't made a plan.

Plan your answer

In the exam, make sure you read the question carefully. Remember to take about five minutes to plan your answer. You'll write a much better essay if you plan it first.

If you had to write an advice sheet for new Year 7s, your plan might look like this:

Mike knew that there had been a plan... a reason for the hat and everything. But he couldn't for the life of him remember what it was.

Plan

Purpose = to advise
Type of writing = advice sheet
Audience = Year 7

• School planner
• Lesson times
• After school activities
• Lunch and break time
• Uniform and equipment
• Homework
• Who to see if you have any problems

1) Your plan should include all the different points you want to cover in your answer.

2) Use your plan to work out the order of your points so your answer flows.

3) Check your plan as you're writing your answer, to make sure you haven't missed anything.

Always start with an Introduction

1) If you're writing an advice sheet or article, write a main heading covering what you're about to write about.

2) Then tell the reader what you're about to advise them about. This is your introduction.

3) Remember who you're advising so you can use the right sort of language for that audience.

4) Talk to the reader directly and try to be reassuring.
Here's an example:

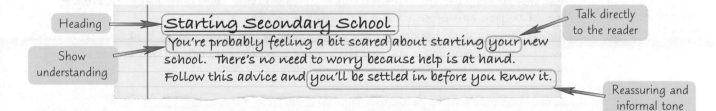

Heading

Show understanding

Starting Secondary School

You're probably feeling a bit scared about starting your new school. There's no need to worry because help is at hand. Follow this advice and you'll be settled in before you know it.

Talk directly to the reader

Reassuring and informal tone

Hmmm... planning looks like as much fun as writing...

Whichever question you do, it's really important to plan what you're going to write. That way, you're not going to miss out any bits you meant to cover. It might feel like you're wasting time by not starting your answer for 5 minutes, but you'll write a better answer in the end.

Writing Your Own

When you're writing to advise, it's important to <u>organise</u> your advice properly.
If it's just a jumble of points, the reader won't be able to take in the information very well.

Organise your Advice

Now it's time to give your advice. The key things to remember are:

1) Use <u>subheadings</u> to separate the main issues you want to cover.

2) <u>Bullet points</u> are really great for <u>separating</u> each point you want to make in a particular section. Make sure you still <u>explain</u> yourself properly though — <u>don't</u> just give a <u>list</u>.

3) And finally, don't forget to finish it off with a <u>conclusion</u> which sums up all your points.

Here's a lovely example of an advice sheet with subheadings and bullet points:

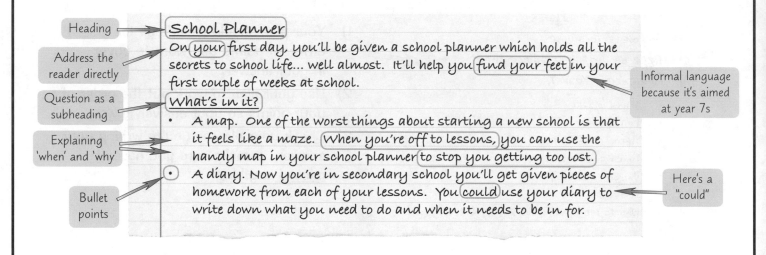

Sum Up your advice at the End

1) Once you've written your advice, all that's left to do is <u>sum up</u> your points.

2) It can often be useful to use <u>bullet points</u>, so the reader can <u>quickly recall</u> the <u>main points</u> of advice without having to read through the whole text again.

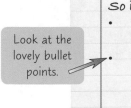

So if you're going to book a holiday, the most important things to remember are:
- You should shop around. The first deal you see might look good but with a bit of browsing you can often find a better deal elsewhere.
- The earlier you book the better. You can get the best holiday deals by booking months in advance. If you leave it until the very last minute there'll be less choice so you'll have to be less fussy about where you go.

Now you can join Agony Aunts Anonymous...

Well, that's it. The fat lady is singing, and you've got to the end of 'how to write to advise'. Keep calm in the exam, plan what you're going to include in your answer, make sure you know who you're writing to, and off you go. Now... I've got this problem... I wonder if you could advise me...

Summary of the Exam

There's just <u>one exam</u> for GCSE <u>English</u> and <u>English Language</u>. It's called <u>Unit 1</u>: Understanding and Producing Non-Fiction Texts. (You take <u>two other</u> units but you do these as <u>controlled assessments</u>.)

The Exam Paper *is* Split Up *like this*

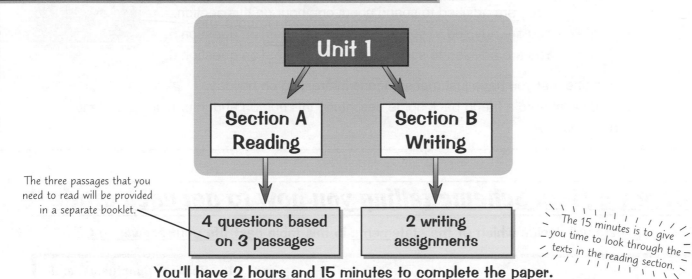

The three passages that you need to read will be provided in a separate booklet.

Unit 1

→ **Section A** Reading → **4 questions based on 3 passages**

→ **Section B** Writing → **2 writing assignments**

You'll have 2 hours and 15 minutes to complete the paper.

The 15 minutes is to give you time to look through the texts in the reading section.

Read *all the* Instructions *on the paper* Before You Start

1) Make sure that you have the <u>foundation paper</u>. It should have a <u>big capital F</u> on the <u>front cover</u>.
2) Before you start, read through <u>all the instructions</u> and advice on the front of the paper.
3) There will be an <u>invigilator</u> (probably one of your teachers) in the exam, who you can <u>ask for help</u> if the instructions aren't clear or you've been given the wrong paper.
4) Fill in all your <u>details</u> (like your <u>name</u> and <u>candidate number</u>) on the <u>front cover</u> of the exam paper.
5) Remember to write all your answers <u>on the pages provided</u> as part of the exam paper.

You must Answer All the Questions *on this paper*

1) For <u>Section A</u> you have to answer all <u>four</u> questions.
2) This section carries <u>40 marks</u> and you're advised to spend <u>one hour</u> on it.
3) <u>Section B</u> requires you to answer <u>both</u> questions, <u>5 and 6</u>.
4) <u>Question 5</u> carries <u>16 marks</u> and should take no more than <u>25 minutes</u>.
5) <u>Question 6</u> carries <u>24 marks</u> and you should spend about <u>35 minutes</u> on it.

- Before you close your paper and sit back and sigh, remember to <u>check</u> back over what you've written.
- This can be a <u>pain</u> after a long exam but you'd be surprised how many <u>silly mistakes</u> you'll spot.
- Try to read through each answer a <u>couple</u> of times and make any <u>corrections</u> as <u>neatly</u> as possible.

Oh — and no talking either...

Knowing what you're in for is half the battle I reckon. There's nothing worse than getting a surprise in an exam so make sure you understand what you're going to have to do before you go in.

Exam Questions — Q5 and Mark Scheme

<u>Section B</u> of your exam paper will look like this:

Don't just answer one of the questions!

Section B: Writing

Answer **both** questions in this section.

You are advised to spend about one hour on this section.

You are advised to spend about 25 minutes on question 5.

You are advised to spend about 35 minutes on question 6.

Don't rush. Spend a few minutes planning your answers.

5   Imagine that you have just met someone interesting on holiday.

Write a letter to a friend back home describing this person and informing your friend how you met.

Here's a Mark Scheme telling you how to get each grade

The <u>examiners</u> will decide which of the <u>statements</u> in this table <u>best fits your answer</u> to Q5.

Grade	What you've written	How you've written	Spelling, punctuation and sentence structures
G/F	Makes a couple of points that are loosely connected to the question, but doesn't really answer the question.	Sentences are simply ordered. The text shows little awareness of the purpose, the audience, or the style of writing required.	Uses simple sentences and basic punctuation. Most basic words are spelt correctly.
E	Makes a few relevant points, but not in any detail. Uses some interesting words and applies simple writing rules, such as always starting a speech with a greeting.	Points are made in a clear order and are sometimes organised into paragraphs. Some awareness of the audience, the purpose, and the style of writing required.	Uses simple sentences with basic spelling and punctuation, and may also include some more complex sentences and spellings.
D	Makes a number of points, some in detail. Chooses simple writing techniques for the right reasons, e.g. using a question in a title to attract interest. Some good vocabulary.	Communicates clearly, using paragraphs to structure work. Fairly good awareness of the audience, the purpose, and the style of writing required.	Uses a wider range of sentence structures and punctuation, e.g. question and exclamation marks. Spelling generally fairly accurate.
C	Makes a number of detailed points in a suitable tone. Uses plenty of interesting vocabulary and a variety of suitable writing techniques effectively.	Points are clearly developed and follow on from one another using linked paragraphs. Shows clear understanding of the purpose, the audience, and the style of writing required.	Uses a variety of sentence structures successfully to produce different effects. Spelling is good, with only the occasional difficult word misspelt. Punctuation is varied and accurate.

Who the heck's Mark Scheme? — and why's he so fussy?

The last page tells you what the exam'll be like. This one tells you what the markers will be looking for in your answer. This stuff is so useful to know it almost feels like cheating (N.B. it's not).

Q5 Grade E & D Answers

Here are some <u>grade E and D</u> exam answers to the question on <u>page 42</u>.

This is a Grade E answer for Question 5

1) Your purpose here is to <u>describe</u>. Remember a description about a person is about their <u>personality</u> as well as what they <u>look</u> like.

2) It will be easier if you describe <u>someone you already know</u> — even if you didn't really meet them on holiday. If you do want to use your imagination though, that's fine.

3) You are writing a letter to a <u>friend</u>, so an <u>informal</u>, <u>chatty</u> tone is great, but don't forget about the <u>spelling</u> and <u>punctuation</u>.

Good opening for a chatty letter.

Watch out for apostrophes.

Hello Jo! I am writing to you from Italy to tell you about someone intresting I met in Italy. I met her at the beach. Her name is Flavia shes a bit older than us with dark hair and brown eyes and she's really nice. You wont believe it but her parents let her ride a moped and my parents let me go on it! I think the sun must of gone to there heads.

Whoops. Make sure you check your spelling — especially if the word is given in the question.

This should say 'must <u>have</u> gone to <u>their</u> heads.'

This is a Grade D answer for Question 5

To improve the grade you'll need to:

1) Try to make your answer a bit <u>exciting</u> by including more <u>detail</u>.

2) Show that you are writing with your <u>audience</u> in mind.

3) Use some more <u>complex sentences</u> and tidy up your <u>spellings</u>.

Luke had learnt the hard way that you don't mess with Bald Eagle.

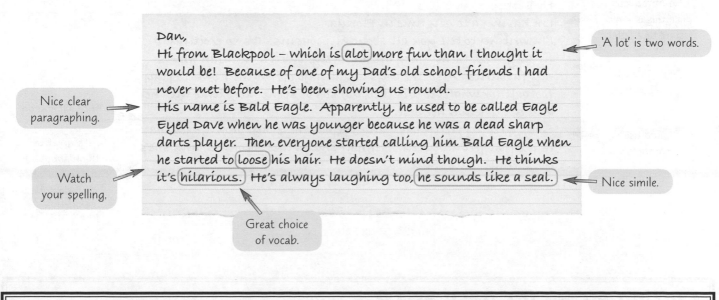

Dan,
Hi from Blackpool – which is alot more fun than I thought it would be! Because of one of my Dad's old school friends I had never met before. He's been showing us round.
His name is Bald Eagle. Apparently, he used to be called Eagle Eyed Dave when he was younger because he was a dead sharp darts player. Then everyone started calling him Bald Eagle when he started to loose his hair. He doesn't mind though. He thinks it's hilarious. He's always laughing too, he sounds like a seal.

Nice clear paragraphing.

Watch your spelling.

Great choice of vocab.

'A lot' is two words.

Nice simile.

The questions do always seem a bit weird, don't they?

It's hard to answer these sort of questions because you'd never normally write to your mates from Peru — or whatever. You've just got to play the examiner's game to get the marks, unfortunately.

Q5 Grade C Answers

So, you've had a look at some grade E and D answers... but we don't want to stop there. No, what you're after is a magical C grade. It's tough, but it's not impossible. This is how you do it.

This is a Grade C answer for Question 5

1) Before you start, re-read the mark scheme so you know what the marker is looking for.
2) Have a think about the differences between a grade D and a grade C.
3) Keep these differences in mind when you're planning and writing your answer.

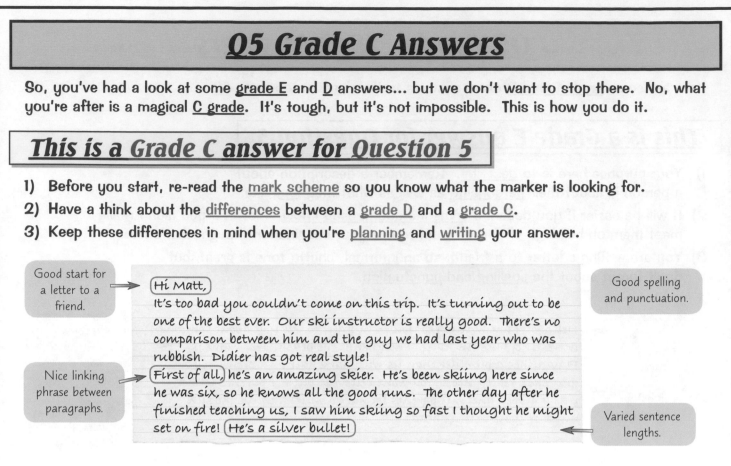

Good start for a letter to a friend.

Hi Matt,
It's too bad you couldn't come on this trip. It's turning out to be one of the best ever. Our ski instructor is really good. There's no comparison between him and the guy we had last year who was rubbish. Didier has got real style!

First of all, he's an amazing skier. He's been skiing here since he was six, so he knows all the good runs. The other day after he finished teaching us, I saw him skiing so fast I thought he might set on fire! He's a silver bullet!

Good spelling and punctuation.

Nice linking phrase between paragraphs.

Varied sentence lengths.

This is a Grade C answer for Question 5

Here's another lovely grade C answer for you. Remember to keep in mind all the things that make a good answer when you're writing, that way you shouldn't go off track.

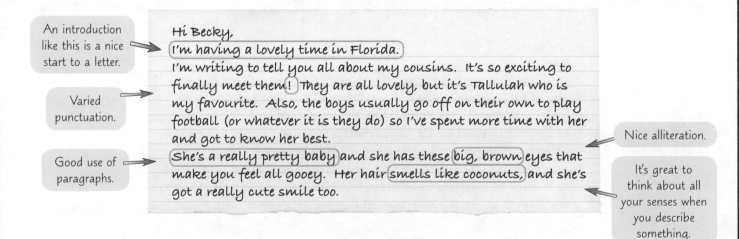

An introduction like this is a nice start to a letter.

Hi Becky,
I'm having a lovely time in Florida.
I'm writing to tell you all about my cousins. It's so exciting to finally meet them! They are all lovely, but it's Tallulah who is my favourite. Also, the boys usually go off on their own to play football (or whatever it is they do) so I've spent more time with her and got to know her best.

She's a really pretty baby and she has these big, brown eyes that make you feel all gooey. Her hair smells like coconuts, and she's got a really cute smile too.

Varied punctuation.

Good use of paragraphs.

Nice alliteration.

It's great to think about all your senses when you describe something.

Getting a C — it's easy as 1,2,3...

So, the magic formula for getting a C... interesting vocabulary, some good writing techniques, paragraphs that flow nicely, a writing style that suits the purpose and audience, some varied sentence structures and accurate spelling and punctuation. Phew. Not much to ask then...

Exam Questions — Q6 and Mark Scheme

After you've wowed the examiners on <u>Question 5</u>, you're just <u>one question</u> short of finishing your exam. All the way from Section B, weighing in at a whopping 24 marks, <u>Question... 6</u>.

You should spend about 35 Minutes on Question 6

1) Remember that you have to answer <u>both</u> questions in <u>section B</u>.

2) There are <u>24 marks</u> up for grabs for <u>Question 6</u>, so it's worth <u>spending a bit longer</u> on.

3) You'll be asked to write something to <u>argue</u>, <u>persuade</u> or <u>advise</u>.

6	Write a script for a radio advertisement to persuade listeners to buy a product or service of your choice.

And here's a little reminder of what the markers are looking for when they read your answers.

Grade	What you've written	How you've written	Spelling, punctuation and sentence structures
G/F	Makes a couple of points that are loosely connected to the question, but doesn't really answer the question.	Sentences are simply ordered. The text shows little awareness of the purpose (to argue, persuade or advise), the audience, or the style of writing required.	Uses simple sentences and basic punctuation. Most basic words are spelt correctly.
E	Makes a few relevant points, but not in any detail. Uses some interesting words and applies simple writing rules, such as always starting a speech with a greeting.	Points are made in a clear order and are sometimes organised into paragraphs. Some awareness of the audience, the purpose (to argue, persuade or advise), and the style of writing required.	Uses simple sentences with basic spelling and punctuation, and may also include some more complex sentences and spellings.
D	Makes a number of points, some in detail. Chooses simple writing techniques for the right reasons, e.g. using a question in a title to attract interest. Some good vocabulary.	Communicates clearly, using paragraphs to structure work. Fairly good awareness of the audience, the purpose (to argue, persuade or advise), and the style of writing required.	Uses a wider range of sentence structures and punctuation, e.g. question and exclamation marks. Spelling generally fairly accurate.
C	Makes a number of detailed points in a suitable tone. Uses plenty of interesting vocabulary and a variety of suitable persuasive writing techniques effectively.	Points are clearly developed and follow on from one another using linked paragraphs. Shows clear understanding of the purpose (to argue, persuade or advise), the audience, and the style of writing required.	Uses a variety of sentence structures successfully to produce different effects. Spelling is good, with only the occasional difficult word misspelt. Punctuation is varied and accurate.

Haven't these markers got anything better to do...

I know it all looks a bit scary when it's written like this, but it's actually not too bad — honest. Have a look at the next couple of pages for some examples of what to do (and what not to do) in the exam.

Q6 Grade E & D Answers

Question 6's all about <u>arguing</u> and <u>persuading</u> people that you're right. There are some useful <u>tricks</u> you can use to make your audience agree with you, so have a gander at these <u>E</u> and <u>D grade</u> answers.

This is a Grade E answer for Question 6

So, your <u>purpose</u> for this question is to <u>persuade</u> somebody to <u>buy</u> something. If you listen to adverts on the radio or telly, there are <u>two things</u> that most of them do:

1) <u>Convince</u> people that the product or service will <u>make their life better</u>.
2) <u>Convince</u> them that it's <u>better</u> than anything their <u>competitors</u> sell.

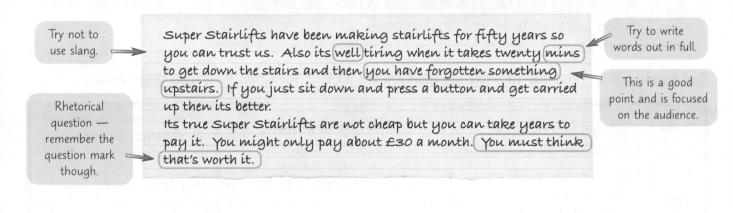

Try not to use slang.

Try to write words out in full.

Rhetorical question — remember the question mark though.

This is a good point and is focused on the audience.

Super Stairlifts have been making stairlifts for fifty years so you can trust us. Also its well tiring when it takes twenty mins to get down the stairs and then you have forgotten something upstairs. If you just sit down and press a button and get carried up then its better.
Its true Super Stairlifts are not cheap but you can take years to pay it. You might only pay about £30 a month. You must think that's worth it.

This is a Grade D answer for Question 6

Let's raise the bar now with a <u>grade D</u> answer. Remember, to get a D you need to:

1) <u>Structure</u> your answer using <u>paragraphs</u>.
2) Use some <u>writing techniques</u> (e.g. alliteration, asking questions).
3) Make sure your <u>spelling</u> and <u>punctuation</u> are quite polished.

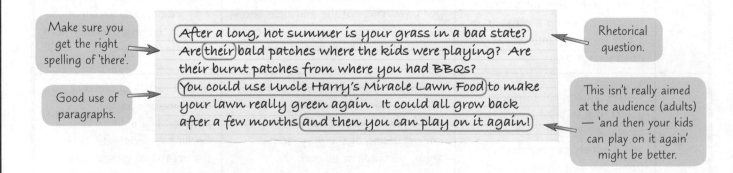

Make sure you get the right spelling of 'there'.

Good use of paragraphs.

Rhetorical question.

This isn't really aimed at the audience (adults) — 'and then your kids can play on it again' might be better.

After a long, hot summer is your grass in a bad state? Are their bald patches where the kids were playing? Are their burnt patches from where you had BBQs?
You could use Uncle Harry's Miracle Lawn Food to make your lawn really green again. It could all grow back after a few months and then you can play on it again!

Stair lifts and lawn food — who said exams were boring...

Actually, these argue and persuade questions can be pretty interesting, because you've got the freedom to come up with anything you like — so if you like football, chances are you can get it in somewhere. The key is to plan what you're going to write, then read through it carefully at the end.

Q6 Grade C Answers

Here it is, the moment you've been waiting for... No, it's not the end of the book. It's far better than that, it's some brilliant <u>grade C</u> answers to <u>question 6</u>.

This is a Grade C answer for Question 6

Remember, to lift your answer to a <u>grade C</u> you need to:

1) Use some good <u>writing techniques</u> and interesting <u>vocabulary</u>.

2) Adapt your <u>writing style</u> to suit the <u>purpose</u> and <u>audience</u>.

3) Make sure your answer is clearly <u>structured</u> and all your <u>paragraphs</u> are well <u>linked</u>.

4) Use different <u>sentence structures</u> and check your <u>spelling</u> and <u>punctuation</u> carefully.

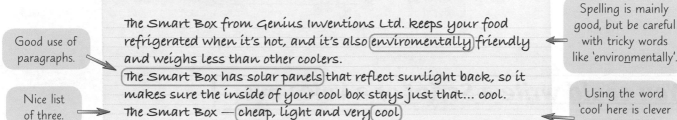

Good use of paragraphs.

Nice list of three.

The Smart Box from Genius Inventions Ltd. keeps your food refrigerated when it's hot, and it's also enviromentally friendly and weighs less than other coolers.
The Smart Box has solar panels that reflect sunlight back, so it makes sure the inside of your cool box stays just that... cool.
The Smart Box — cheap, light and very cool

Spelling is mainly good, but be careful with tricky words like 'environmentally'.

Using the word 'cool' here is clever because it has a double meaning.

This is a Grade C answer for Question 6

Hopefully you've got the hang of it now, but just to make sure, here's a final top-notch <u>grade C</u> answer for you.

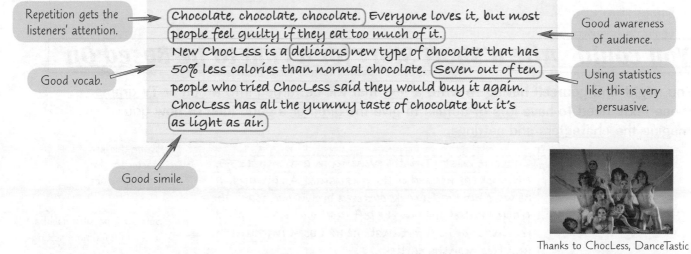

Repetition gets the listeners' attention.

Good vocab.

Good simile.

Chocolate, chocolate, chocolate. Everyone loves it, but most people feel guilty if they eat too much of it.
New ChocLess is a delicious new type of chocolate that has 50% less calories than normal chocolate. Seven out of ten people who tried ChocLess said they would buy it again. ChocLess has all the yummy taste of chocolate but it's as light as air.

Good awareness of audience.

Using statistics like this is very persuasive.

Thanks to ChocLess, DanceTastic could now wear their skimpiest outfits without unsightly bulges.

Mmmm, chocolate — that's more like it...

So that's it, your all-singing, all-dancing guide to how to do well in your exam. The main thing is just to stay calm, think carefully before you start writing and try to include some of the things that the markers love so much — like paragraphs, good spelling and a smattering of writing techniques.

Writing About Moving Images

Writing about what? It just means 'Writing about <u>movies</u> and <u>TV shows</u>' — sounds like fun.

You might have to Write a Film Review

1) You'll need to provide <u>facts</u> about the film — e.g. what it's about and how long it is.

2) You also need to think about <u>who you're writing for</u> and whether you think <u>they'd</u> enjoy the film.

3) <u>Persuasive language</u> is useful if you're trying to <u>convince</u> people to go and see it.

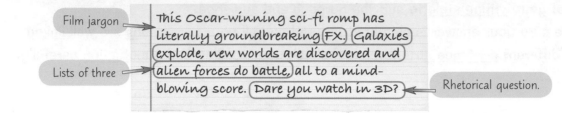

Film jargon → This Oscar-winning sci-fi romp has literally groundbreaking (FX.) (Galaxies explode, new worlds are discovered and alien forces do battle,) all to a mind-blowing score. (Dare you watch in 3D?)

Lists of three

Rhetorical question.

You could write a Script or a Voice-over

<u>Voice-overs</u> and <u>scripts</u> for dialogue pop up all over — in <u>soaps</u>, <u>cartoons</u>, <u>adverts</u> and <u>documentaries</u>.
You need to <u>change</u> the tone to suit the <u>purpose</u> of your piece.

underwater, daytime:
voice-over:

(Blind fish swimming)
Isolated for generations in a network of caves beneath the Rio Grande, the Mexican Tetra has developed several unique adaptations to life in a world without light. (These creatures have no eyes and each one is pinkish-white...)

Show what viewers would see.

Documentary scripts give the voice-over person plenty of chances to take a breath.

Offer lots of information.

You could write a Short Story for a Film to be Based On

You might find yourself having to write a <u>text</u> that will be <u>turned into</u> a <u>film</u> or <u>TV drama</u>.
These texts need to have <u>lots of details</u> to give the <u>director</u> a good idea of how you
imagine the <u>characters</u> and <u>settings</u>.

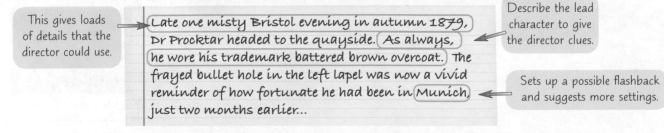

This gives loads of details that the director could use.

Late one misty Bristol evening in autumn 1879, Dr Procktar headed to the quayside. (As always,) he wore his trademark battered brown overcoat.) The frayed bullet hole in the left lapel was now a vivid reminder of how fortunate he had been in (Munich,) just two months earlier...

Describe the lead character to give the director clues.

Sets up a possible flashback and suggests more settings.

Battle Royale — based on a true story...

If a picture says a thousand words and a film is shot at 24 frames a second and lasts 162 minutes
— I make that two hundred and thirty three million, two hundred and eighty thousand words. Woah.

Writing on a Particular Theme

You might choose to do a 'commissions' piece if you're taking English Language. If you're taking English, you might choose a 'prompts' question. Either way, you could have to write on a theme.

Some Themes are Open to Interpretation

1) You might be asked to write on a theme that the examiners have made a bit vague.

2) They could use words that have more than one meaning, or use really broad topics.

3) The question below is an example of the sort of thing you might get.

> Write a creative piece on the theme 'The Four Seasons'

4) There's probably a few things that spring to mind straight away — so scribble them down.

5) Once you've jotted down all you can think of, you can decide which idea you want to write about.

6) When you've made your mind up, you can start thinking about the purpose of your text, what form it'll take and who you're writing it for.

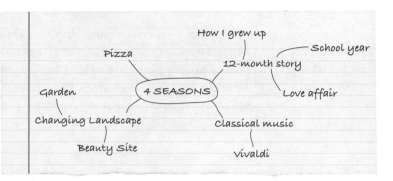

Other Themes can be a lot more Specific

1) You might choose a task where you have to do a particular type of creative writing.

2) On these types of question, you don't really have to interpret the theme and your purpose, form or audience may have already been decided for you.

3) Have a look at the questions below for an idea of the kinds of things you might get:

> Write a story beginning with the line:
> "That's the last time I ever …', said X'

Purpose: describe/inform/entertain
Form: story about an incident
Audience: general readers

> Write a hobby-based article for your school or club website.

Purpose: inform (& persuade?)
Form: Online article, with lots of facts
Audience: School community / visitors

It's easier than writing about Ham and Pineapple...

Being asked to 'write on a theme' is a bit scary. But if you plan your answer before you start writing and always bear in mind your purpose, form and audience, you can't go too far wrong.

Changing the Genre of a Text

Believe it or not, changing a text's genre can actually be quite fun. I expect that you have chosen not to believe it, but you'll need to be able to do it anyway — so you may as well read this page...

You might change a Play or Poem into a Short Story...

1) Turning a piece into a short story gives you the chance to add to the original text.
2) You could use the speech, characters and stage directions from plays, or the feelings and themes from a poem.
3) Remember to think about the point of view — e.g. you could change it so it's written from the point of view of one of the characters.
4) You could also change the tense — e.g. re-write something so it's in the past tense.
5) Here's an example of how you could change a scene from Macbeth into a short story:

Extra details add excitement to your story.

"Why did you bring these daggers from the place?" hissed Lady Macbeth, glaring at the sight of her husband's crimson hands, and making no effort to hide her impatience with him. Macbeth's gaze drifted from her stern brow to the weapon trembling in his palm as though trying to free itself from his twisted fingers...

You could use actual lines from the play or you can change them.

... or change a Text into a Non-Fiction Piece

1) Non-fiction texts are things like articles, leaflets or radio broadcasts.
2) The example below shows how the events in 'Of Mice and Men' could be turned into a newspaper article:

The headline is appropriate for a newspaper article.

RANCH WORKER FOUND DEAD AFTER CORPSE DISCOVERY
Details are emerging after two bodies were found near Soledad yesterday. The first, the body of a young female, was found in a barn in the late afternoon. Less than an hour after the discovery of the woman, a second fatality was reported in an area of woodland just three quarters of a mile away. Authorities have not released the identities of the bodies but it is understood that the deaths are both being treated as suspicious, and are believed to be linked in some way.

Details from the original text show that you understand it.

A formal tone like this is appropriate.

Crime reports always include lots of facts.

Phrases like this make the article seem like proper journalism

Adapt the text to a script for 'George and Lennie On Ice'...

This may be hard to come to terms with — but, all the fun stuff, like making your text look like the front page of a newspaper, doesn't count for any marks in the assessment so don't waste time on it.

Writing From Your Point of View

Writing from your <u>own</u> point of view is really important if you're doing <u>English</u>.
If you're doing <u>English Language</u>, the controlled assessments are less focused
on it — but it's still a <u>really useful skill</u> so stick around...

You might write about a Memory or a Personal Opinion

If you're writing from your <u>own viewpoint</u> you still need to think about <u>who</u> you're writing for,
and the <u>purpose</u> of the piece. If you can write in any <u>form</u>, think about what's best for <u>getting
your feelings across</u>.

1) If you're writing about your personal <u>opinions</u>, think about the
<u>details</u> or <u>events</u> that led you to have that point of view.

2) Include lots of <u>personal stories</u>. You can <u>make them up</u> if you like
but it's easier if you've got some real ones that you could <u>relate</u> to.

3) Try not to be <u>shy</u> about showing <u>emotion</u>, <u>warmth</u> or <u>pain</u>. If you
feel strongly about something, let it come across in your writing.
It'll probably make your piece a lot more <u>powerful</u>.

4) If you're <u>describing</u> something, like a <u>place</u> or a <u>person</u>, use your
different <u>senses</u>. Think about <u>sounds</u>, <u>smells</u>, <u>textures</u> and <u>tastes</u>
as well as how things <u>look</u>.

Have a look at these Example Tasks

Some forms are really well-suited for getting personal feelings across — e.g. <u>blogs</u>, <u>diary entries</u>,
<u>speeches</u>. You could also write a <u>short story</u> or <u>'real-life' magazine article</u> — see below:

Write about what, in your experience, makes a good friend.

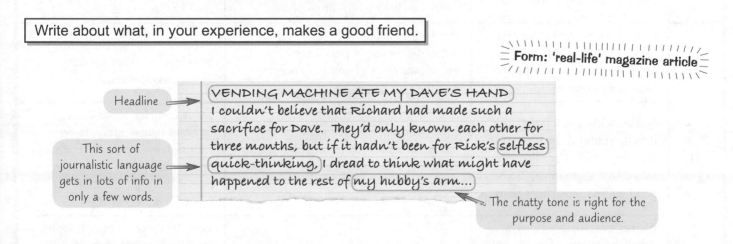

Form: 'real-life' magazine article

Headline →

VENDING MACHINE ATE MY DAVE'S HAND
I couldn't believe that Richard had made such a
sacrifice for Dave. They'd only known each other for
three months, but if it hadn't been for Rick's selfless
quick-thinking, I dread to think what might have
happened to the rest of my hubby's arm...

This sort of journalistic language gets in lots of info in only a few words.

The chatty tone is right for the purpose and audience.

This one time, at band camp...

When you tackle one of these questions, try and remember the four points in the purple box.
At least this is one type of question where you've got no excuse for factual inaccuracies...

What You Have To Do — English Language

Your Unit 3b controlled assessment is like a cross between coursework and an exam. It might not be much fun, but it does count for 15% of your overall GCSE, so it's worth doing well.

You get a Choice of Tasks for the Controlled Assessment

1) You have to do two pieces of creative writing, chosen from a bank of six topics.

2) There are three topics, and two tasks for each. The topics are:
   - 'Moving Images' — writing for or about moving images (e.g. film reviews or scripts).
   - 'Commissions' — writing to a brief (e.g. a magazine article or website content).
   - 'Re-creations' — taking a text you already know and turning it into something different.

3) You'll have up to 4 hours to write about 1200 words in total for the two pieces — they don't have to be of equal length (e.g. one could be 500 words and one could be 700 words).

4) You can use 'brief notes' during the final write-up, but not a whole draft.

5) You can use resources like the internet while you're preparing, but not during the write-up.

6) Each piece is marked out of 10 for structure and content, and there are 10 more marks for accuracy.

Here's a Mark Scheme telling you how to get each grade

This mark scheme shows what the markers look for when deciding which grade to give your piece of creative genius. They'll work out which of the statements in this table best fits your work.

Grade	What you've written	How you've written	Spelling, punctuation and sentence structures
F	Makes a few simple points without much depth or detail. Some awareness of form.	Sentences follow on from one another simply (e.g. using 'and then'). Not much matching of writing style with purpose or audience. Paragraphs often ignored.	Uses simple sentences and basic punctuation. Most basic words spelt correctly. Some effort to spell harder words.
E	Makes a few points that relate directly to the question. Uses simple writing techniques. Interesting words sometimes used.	Points are made in clear but simple order. Some use of paragraphs. Some awareness of audience, purpose and the type of writing.	Written in complete sentences. Simple words spelt correctly. Good basic punctuation.
D	Makes quite a few points that directly relate to the question, some in detail. Words used suited to the audience. Some good writing techniques used.	Clearly written. Sometimes uses paragraphs correctly to organise writing. The writer's mostly aware of the purpose, audience and type of writing.	Some complex sentences. Spelling mainly accurate even with unfamiliar words. Full stops and capital letters used correctly. Some varied punctuation, e.g. question marks, used.
C	Makes clear, detailed points using correct style for purpose and audience. Good vocabulary and techniques used (e.g. alliteration). Interesting to read with depth and detail included.	Piece has a clear structure and paragraphs follow on from each other. A clear understanding of the purpose, audience and style of writing.	Uses sentences effectively, both short and longer. Simple and complex spelling nearly always correct. Good range of accurate punctuation, e.g. speech or exclamation marks, used for effect.

Moving Images — Grade E & D Answers

Here are some examples of the kinds of task you might get, with grade E and D answers to them.

1) For this topic you'll have to write something <u>for</u> or <u>about</u> 'Moving Images'.

2) This means you'll have to think about the <u>pictures</u> that your language will <u>describe</u> or <u>create</u>, so you should include lots of <u>interesting description</u>.

3) Make sure you have a clear plan in your head before you start — think about your <u>purpose</u>, <u>form</u> and <u>audience</u>.

Here's a Sample Task and Grade E answer

> Write the 'voice-over' script for a documentary about bullying.
> Show how your writing relates to the images in your documentary.

This answer needs more description to show what the viewers would see.

Rhetorical question, but it needs a question mark.

Bullying is terrible. I want to explain why people should be a lot kinder to other people. If you treat people like you want to be treated then ul be a better person and ul go to heaven. Standing outside the school gates b4 hometime you can see people hit and shout at people. This one time I saw two girls picking on someone until they made her cry and that was when the teacher came out to stop them. Should teachers get involved. Sometimes it can make it worse like when the bullys think that you've told the teacher about them when acshally you have'nt and its just that the teacher knows anyway.

Outlines the aim well.

Don't use text speak in your answers.

Check your spelling and punctuation carefully.

Here's a Sample Task and Grade D answer

> Write a newspaper review of a television programme.

Nice alliteration.

Rhetorical question.

'A Perfect Murder' Review
Sunday nights neednt be dull. That's because a new whodunnit series has started on Channel 14 which is clever, well acted and keeps you watching. Its perfect for sleepy Sunday veiwing.
The new summer series stars the awesome Chester Layborne as mavveric journalist Tony Black and his posh assistant Carla who adds glammer and pazazz to the show. They solve crimes like murders that the police can't solve because they look at things in a different way and do things that the police aren't allowed to do.
I often wonder, could this happen in real life? Sometimes the plot is so ridiculous and funny that you don't believe it but it doesn't stop me from enjoying its twists and turns while I finish my homework.
If you want something light for Sunday night and don't mind that its a bit silly then this is the show for you!

Interesting vocab, but be careful with your spelling.

This sentence needs some punctuation.

A strong ending to the review.

Moving Images — Grade C Answers

Have a good look at these answers and the comments next to them. They show you the kind of interesting <u>language</u> and <u>writing techniques</u> you need to include in your answers to get a <u>C</u>.

Here's a Sample Task and Grade C answer

> Write the 'voice-over' script for a video podcast about the environment.
> Think about how your text relates to the areas and images you would choose to show.

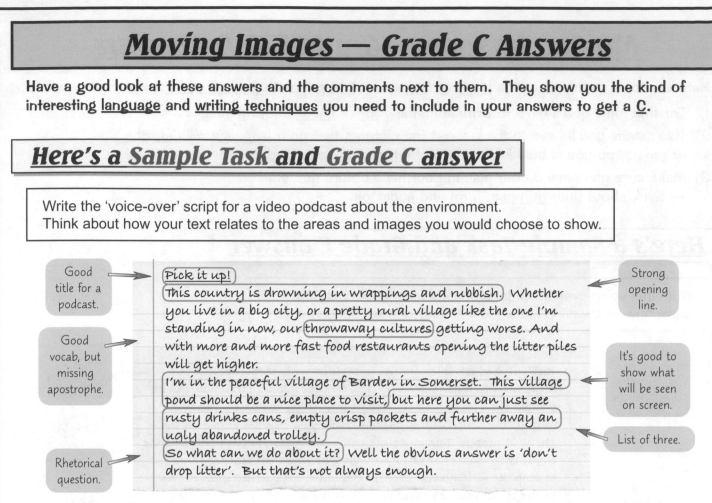

Good title for a podcast. →

Pick it up!
This country is drowning in wrappings and rubbish. Whether you live in a big city, or a pretty rural village like the one I'm standing in now, our throwaway cultures getting worse. And with more and more fast food restaurants opening the litter piles will get higher.

Good vocab, but missing apostrophe. →

I'm in the peaceful village of Barden in Somerset. This village pond should be a nice place to visit, but here you can just see rusty drinks cans, empty crisp packets and further away an ugly abandoned trolley.

Rhetorical question. →

So what can we do about it? Well the obvious answer is 'don't drop litter'. But that's not always enough.

← Strong opening line.

← It's good to show what will be seen on screen.

← List of three.

Here's a Sample Task and Grade C answer

> Write a letter to a friend in which you review a film you have seen.

An informal opening is appropriate for a friend. →

Hello Carrie,
It's been absolutely ages since I contacted you (I'm so sorry), but I've been madly busy this summer and haven't had time to think, let alone write a letter.
Busy with what, I hear you ask? Well, I've been watching loads of classic films and have become so interested in them that I often forget to eat (as if I'm in another world).

Good linking of paragraphs. →

Speaking of other worlds, I just had to tell you about one film that I know you'd love — Moths and Moonbeams. Even if you've read the book, when you see it in hi-res 3D, you enter a truly magical fantasy land. The enchanted forest and the Lake of Souls were done exactly as I imagined them, and the scene with the harpies was even more scary than in the book! Better still, it stars Jesse Markham (swoon!).

Interesting vocabulary. →

I know you're not really a fan, but he's amazing in this, and his transformation is breathtaking (I won't say any more because I don't want to spoil it!). Lena Lowden is as mad as a hatter so she's perfect as the cruel, cold but beautiful fairy queen with a dark secret...

List of three. →

← Using a variety of sentence structures adds interest.

← It's good to use film jargon.

← Good use of simile.

Commissions — Grade E & D Answers

Right, a quick change of topic now, but the same mark scheme (on page 52) applies.
Here are two more lovely <u>tasks</u> and examples of <u>E</u> and <u>D grade answers</u> for you to read.

1) For this topic you'll be given a <u>commission</u> that you have to write something <u>for</u>.
2) It's like being a famous writer who's been asked to write something for a particular <u>reason</u>.
3) Remember to get your answer clear in your head <u>before</u> you start — so think about your <u>purpose</u>, <u>form</u> and <u>audience</u>.

Here's a Sample Task and Grade E answer

You have been asked by your headteacher to write a speech for a school assembly with the title 'Exams'.

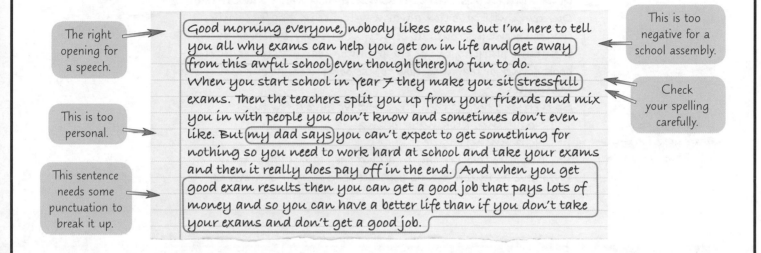

The right opening for a speech.

This is too personal.

This sentence needs some punctuation to break it up.

Good morning everyone, nobody likes exams but I'm here to tell you all why exams can help you get on in life and get away from this awful school even though there no fun to do.
When you start school in Year 7 they make you sit stressfull exams. Then the teachers split you up from your friends and mix you in with people you don't know and sometimes don't even like. But my dad says you can't expect to get something for nothing so you need to work hard at school and take your exams and then it really does pay off in the end. And when you get good exam results then you can get a good job that pays lots of money and so you can have a better life than if you don't take your exams and don't get a good job.

This is too negative for a school assembly.

Check your spelling carefully.

Here's a Sample Task and Grade D answer

You've been asked by a student magazine to write a new feature called 'Change Must Happen'.
Write in any form about an issue you think is important to teenagers.

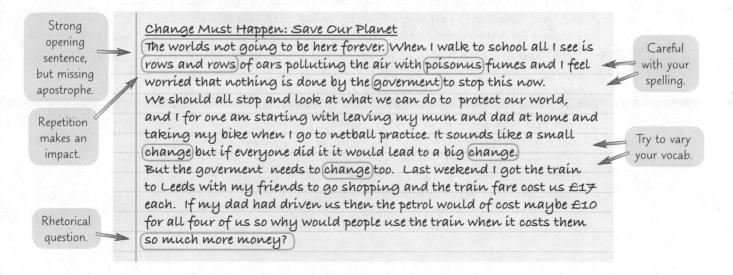

Strong opening sentence, but missing apostrophe.

Repetition makes an impact.

Rhetorical question.

Change Must Happen: Save Our Planet
The worlds not going to be here forever. When I walk to school all I see is rows and rows of cars polluting the air with poisonus fumes and I feel worried that nothing is done by the goverment to stop this now.
We should all stop and look at what we can do to protect our world, and I for one am starting with leaving my mum and dad at home and taking my bike when I go to netball practice. It sounds like a small change but if everyone did it it would lead to a big change.
But the goverment needs to change too. Last weekend I got the train to Leeds with my friends to go shopping and the train fare cost us £17 each. If my dad had driven us then the petrol would of cost maybe £10 for all four of us so why would people use the train when it costs them so much more money?

Careful with your spelling.

Try to vary your vocab.

Commissions — Grade C Answers

Time to look at two <u>C grade</u> responses so you can get the hang of what good things to include in your answers. You'll have to go that extra mile with some winning writing but it really can be done.

Here's a Sample Task and Grade C answer

> You have been asked to write an 'About Us' section for the website of a local business. You are free to decide what the company produces or offers.

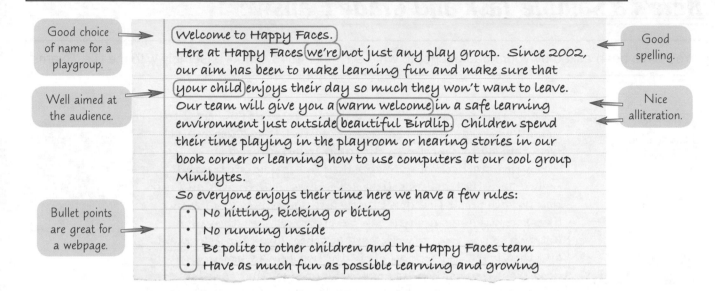

Good choice of name for a playgroup.

Well aimed at the audience.

Bullet points are great for a webpage.

Good spelling.

Nice alliteration.

Welcome to Happy Faces.
Here at Happy Faces we're not just any play group. Since 2002, our aim has been to make learning fun and make sure that your child enjoys their day so much they won't want to leave. Our team will give you a warm welcome in a safe learning environment just outside beautiful Birdlip. Children spend their time playing in the playroom or hearing stories in our book corner or learning how to use computers at our cool group Minibytes.
So everyone enjoys their time here we have a few rules:
- No hitting, kicking or biting
- No running inside
- Be polite to other children and the Happy Faces team
- Have as much fun as possible learning and growing

Here's a Sample Task and Grade C answer

> You've been asked to write an article for a magazine which will feature in their 'Family' pages. You can write about any issue that you feel is appropriate.

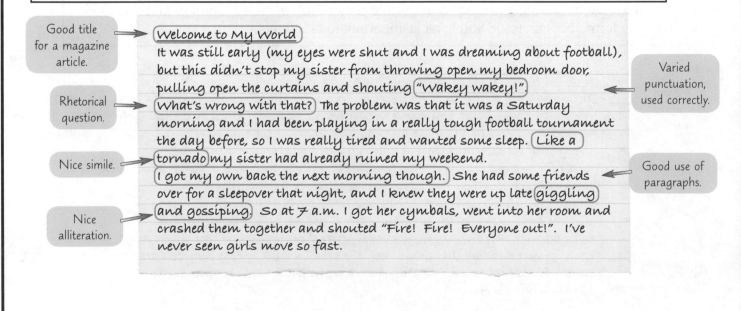

Good title for a magazine article.

Rhetorical question.

Nice simile.

Nice alliteration.

Varied punctuation, used correctly.

Good use of paragraphs.

Welcome to My World
It was still early (my eyes were shut and I was dreaming about football), but this didn't stop my sister from throwing open my bedroom door, pulling open the curtains and shouting "Wakey wakey!". What's wrong with that? The problem was that it was a Saturday morning and I had been playing in a really tough football tournament the day before, so I was really tired and wanted some sleep. Like a tornado my sister had already ruined my weekend.
I got my own back the next morning though. She had some friends over for a sleepover that night, and I knew they were up late giggling and gossiping. So at 7 a.m. I got her cymbals, went into her room and crashed them together and shouted "Fire! Fire! Everyone out!". I've never seen girls move so fast.

Re-creations — Grade E & D Answers

Now you've got the hang of it, here's another change of topic and a couple of <u>E</u> and <u>D grade answers</u> for you to see exactly <u>how</u> grades are <u>earned</u> (nothing to do with whether the marker's having a bad day).

1) This topic asks you to change a <u>text you know</u> into something <u>different</u>.

2) You might be asked to <u>change</u> a scene from a <u>play</u>, a chapter from a <u>novel</u> or a <u>poem</u> into <u>another type</u> of writing.

Here's a Sample Task and Grade E answer

Transform a key scene from a play you have read into a piece of non-fiction or journalistic writing.

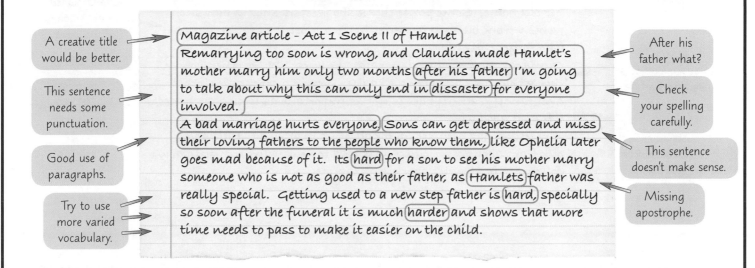

A creative title would be better.

This sentence needs some punctuation.

Good use of paragraphs.

Try to use more varied vocabulary.

Magazine article - Act 1 Scene II of Hamlet
Remarrying too soon is wrong, and Claudius made Hamlet's mother marry him only two months after his father I'm going to talk about why this can only end in dissaster for everyone involved.
A bad marriage hurts everyone. Sons can get depressed and miss their loving fathers to the people who know them, like Ophelia later goes mad because of it. Its hard for a son to see his mother marry someone who is not as good as their father, as Hamlets father was really special. Getting used to a new step father is hard, specially so soon after the funeral it is much harder and shows that more time needs to pass to make it easier on the child.

After his father what?

Check your spelling carefully.

This sentence doesn't make sense.

Missing apostrophe.

Here's a Sample Task and Grade D answer

Read the poem 'The Hunchback in the Park' by Dylan Thomas from the Character and Voice section of the AQA Anthology. Transform it into a non-fiction or journalistic piece.

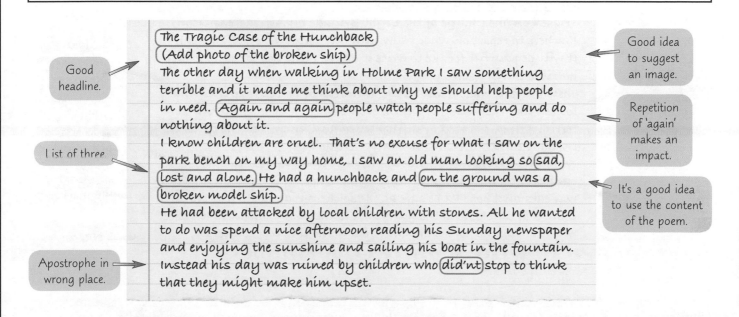

Good headline.

List of three.

Apostrophe in wrong place.

The Tragic Case of the Hunchback
(Add photo of the broken ship)
The other day when walking in Holme Park I saw something terrible and it made me think about why we should help people in need. Again and again people watch people suffering and do nothing about it.
I know children are cruel. That's no excuse for what I saw on the park bench on my way home, I saw an old man looking so sad, lost and alone. He had a hunchback and on the ground was a broken model ship.
He had been attacked by local children with stones. All he wanted to do was spend a nice afternoon reading his Sunday newspaper and enjoying the sunshine and sailing his boat in the fountain. Instead his day was ruined by children who did'nt stop to think that they might make him upset.

Good idea to suggest an image.

Repetition of 'again' makes an impact.

It's a good idea to use the content of the poem.

Re-creations — Grade C Answers

Let's take it up another level and see what a top notch <u>C grade</u> answer needs to include. Even if you're <u>not</u> aiming for a C, you can still pick up some handy <u>hints</u> from reading these <u>examples</u>.

Here's a Sample Task and Grade C answer

> Read the poem 'The Ruined Maid' by Thomas Hardy from the Character and Voice section of the AQA Anthology. Transform this poem into a newspaper article.

Good title for a newspaper article.

It's a great idea to add quotes to a newspaper article.

Nice alliteration, and uses detail from the poem.

Old-fashioned vocab is good for this piece.

Local Girl Stuns Village
Villagers were shocked when they spotted Melia Howell back in her old home. Some people think shopkeepers should ban such women from buying groceries to prove a point to fallen women who forget their morals.
Our vicar, Reverend Loxley, said "We must not let other women think that it's OK to behave badly. Wearing expensive clothes and fancy feathery hats is not as important as living an honest life as a good wife."
A meeting has been set up for all of us to attend to talk about our fears about our young girls and to make sure our girls don't follow Melia Howell's shocking example.

Here's a Sample Task and Grade C answer

> Look at the poems in the Conflict section of the AQA Anthology.
> Transform one of these poems into an eye-witness account based on the content or ideas presented.

It's good to use detail and imagery from the poem.

Onomatopoeia.

Nice alliteration.

Adding historical detail is a great idea.

Good metaphor.

Nice simile.

News from the Front, October 1854
(Based on The Charge of the Light Brigade by Alfred Tennyson)
I'm here to report on what I saw with my very own eyes. Though it will be painful for me to write it down, I will try to record every horrible thing I saw.
Their bravery was shown as the hundreds of heroes rode into what looked like the valley of Death, even though all the soldiers were terribly tired, worried and frightened and knew that the generals in charge didn't know what they were doing.
There was terrifying silence as the men lined up ready. The cannons boomed so loudly that I had to hold my hands against my ears and hope I'd be safe as the soldiers rode out to hell on earth. Clouds of smoke and the guns shot louder than thunder. It broke my heart as the horses and men fell down like toy soldiers.

What You Have To Do — English

Your <u>Unit 3b</u> <u>controlled assessment</u> is like a <u>cross</u> between coursework and an exam.
It might not be much fun, but it does count for <u>20%</u> of your <u>overall GCSE</u>, so it's worth doing well.

You get a Choice of Tasks for the Controlled Assessment

1) You have to do <u>two pieces</u> of <u>creative writing</u>, chosen from a <u>bank of six topics</u>.

2) There are <u>three topics</u>, and <u>two tasks</u> for each. The topics are:
   - <u>'Moving Images'</u> — writing <u>for</u> or <u>about</u> moving images (e.g. film reviews or scripts).
   - <u>'Prompts and Re-creations'</u> — using a <u>text</u> or <u>statement</u> as a <u>cue</u> for your own writing.
   - <u>'Me. Myself. I.'</u> — writing creatively about something <u>you've done</u>, <u>felt</u> or <u>experienced</u>.

3) You'll have <u>up to 4 hours</u> to write about <u>1600 words</u> in total for the two pieces — they <u>don't</u> have to be of <u>equal length</u> (e.g. one could be 900 words and one could be 700 words).

4) You can use <u>'brief notes'</u> during the final write-up, but <u>not</u> a whole draft.

5) You can use <u>resources</u> like the internet while you're <u>preparing</u>, but <u>not</u> during the write-up.

6) Each piece is marked out of <u>15</u> for <u>structure</u> and <u>content</u>, and there are <u>15</u> more marks for <u>accuracy</u>.

Here's a Mark Scheme telling you how to get each grade

This <u>mark scheme</u> shows what the <u>markers</u> look for when deciding which grade to give your piece of creative genius. They'll work out which of the <u>statements</u> in this table <u>best fits your work</u>.

Grade	What you've written	How you've written	Spelling, punctuation and sentence structures
F	Makes a few simple points without much depth or detail. Some awareness of form.	Sentences follow on from one another simply (e.g. using 'and then'). Not much matching of writing style with purpose or audience. Paragraphs often ignored.	Uses simple sentences and basic punctuation. Most basic words spelt correctly. Some effort to spell harder words.
E	Makes a few points that relate directly to the question. Uses simple writing techniques. Interesting words sometimes used.	Points are made in clear but simple order. Some use of paragraphs. Some awareness of audience, purpose and the type of writing.	Written in complete sentences. Simple words spelt correctly. Good basic punctuation.
D	Makes quite a few points that directly relate to the question, some in detail. Words used suited to the audience. Some good writing techniques used.	Clearly written. Sometimes uses paragraphs correctly to organise writing. The writer's mostly aware of the purpose, audience and type of writing.	Some complex sentences. Spelling mainly accurate even with unfamiliar words. Full stops and capital letters used correctly. Some varied punctuation, e.g. question marks, used.
C	Makes clear, detailed points using correct style for purpose and audience. Good vocabulary and techniques used (e.g. alliteration). Interesting to read with depth and detail included.	Piece has a clear structure and paragraphs follow on from each other. A clear understanding of the purpose, audience and style of writing.	Uses sentences effectively, both short and longer. Simple and complex spelling nearly always correct. Good range of accurate punctuation, e.g. speech or exclamation marks, used for effect.

Moving Images — Grade E & D Answers

It's time to take a look at some examples of tasks and two <u>E</u> and <u>D grade answers</u> to them.

1) For this topic you'll have to write something <u>for</u> or <u>about</u> 'Moving Images'.

2) This means you'll have to think about the <u>pictures</u> that your language will <u>describe</u> or <u>create</u>.

3) Include lots of <u>interesting description</u> to create <u>pictures</u> in your reader's mind.

4) Make sure you have a clear plan in your head before you start — think about your <u>purpose</u>, <u>form</u> and <u>audience</u>.

Here's a Sample Task and Grade E answer

Pick a key scene from a television programme you have watched and write a descriptive piece which captures the same atmosphere as the original scene.

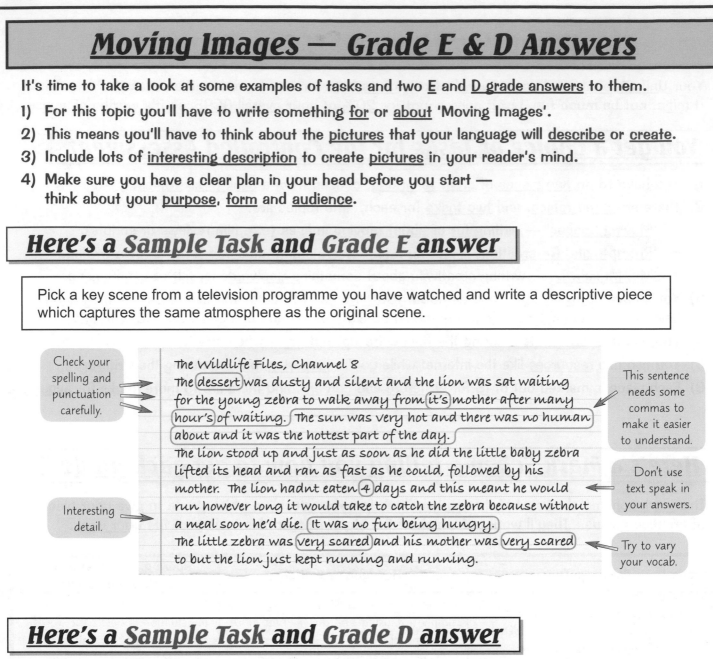

Check your spelling and punctuation carefully.

The Wildlife Files, Channel 8
The (dessert) was dusty and silent and the lion was sat waiting for the young zebra to walk away from (it's) mother after many (hour's) of waiting. The sun was very hot and there was no human about and it was the hottest part of the day.
The lion stood up and just as soon as he did the little baby zebra lifted its head and ran as fast as he could, followed by his mother. The lion hadnt eaten (4) days and this meant he would run however long it would take to catch the zebra because without a meal soon he'd die. (It was no fun being hungry.)
The little zebra was (very scared) and his mother was (very scared) to but the lion just kept running and running.

This sentence needs some commas to make it easier to understand.

Don't use text speak in your answers.

Interesting detail.

Try to vary your vocab.

Here's a Sample Task and Grade D answer

Develop your own ending to a film you have seen.
Try to capture the atmosphere of the original and include visual detail.

Good clear title.

'Sinking Deeper' — The Alternative Ending
As the sun came up he blinked and slowly opened the blinds, not sure what he would see and waiting for a sign. The air smelt of stale (fag) smoke and the room was the cheapest he could get with scratchy sheets and dust and mess everywhere. His wife (wouldn't of) liked it and he was glad she was'nt here, even though he missed her.
Suddenly he could see a car driving towards him in the (distance) (getting faster and noisier) as it got closer to his motel. He closed his eyes and hoped that the car was Eddie here to take him away, but when he opened them again he saw the angry driver and (flasshing) blue lights and he knew he had been found. He knew that this time he'd be locked up and they'd throw away the key. (Was there any hope for him?)

Don't use too much slang.

Should be 'wouldn't have', not 'wouldn't of'.

Good visual detail, and it's good to describe what you'd hear too.

Check your spelling carefully.

Rhetorical question.

Moving Images — Grade C Answers

Getting a <u>C grade</u> is no easy task, but there's no great mystery involved. Have a good read of these <u>sample answers</u> and <u>comments</u> to see the kind of writing that you should be producing.

Here's a Sample Task and Grade C answer

Write a short story that could be the basis for the opening scene of a war film. Include visual detail to keep the audience interested.

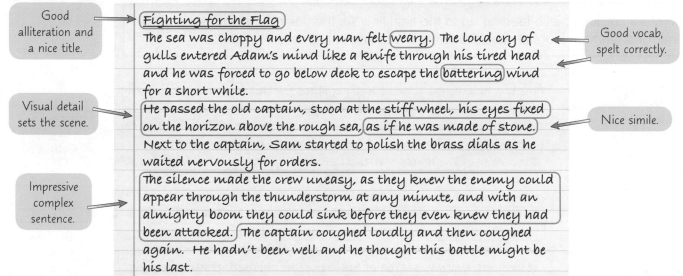

Good alliteration and a nice title.

Visual detail sets the scene.

Impressive complex sentence.

Good vocab, spelt correctly.

Nice simile.

> Fighting for the Flag
> The sea was choppy and every man felt weary. The loud cry of gulls entered Adam's mind like a knife through his tired head and he was forced to go below deck to escape the battering wind for a short while.
> He passed the old captain, stood at the stiff wheel, his eyes fixed on the horizon above the rough sea, as if he was made of stone. Next to the captain, Sam started to polish the brass dials as he waited nervously for orders.
> The silence made the crew uneasy, as they knew the enemy could appear through the thunderstorm at any minute, and with an almighty boom they could sink before they even knew they had been attacked. The captain coughed loudly and then coughed again. He hadn't been well and he thought this battle might be his last.

Here's a Sample Task and Grade C answer

Write a short story that could form the basis of a film. You can focus on a key scene. Include visual detail and create atmosphere for the audience.

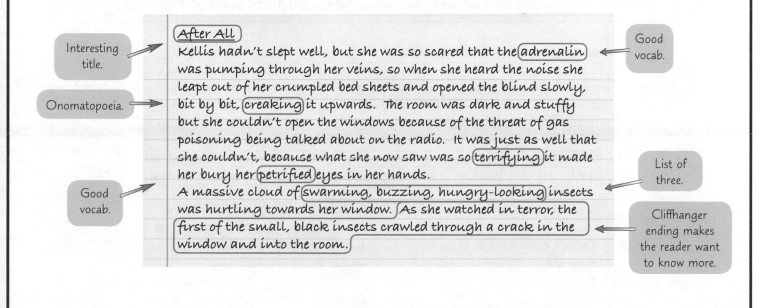

Interesting title.

Onomatopoeia.

Good vocab.

Good vocab.

List of three.

Cliffhanger ending makes the reader want to know more.

> After All
> Kellis hadn't slept well, but she was so scared that the adrenalin was pumping through her veins, so when she heard the noise she leapt out of her crumpled bed sheets and opened the blind slowly, bit by bit, creaking it upwards. The room was dark and stuffy but she couldn't open the windows because of the threat of gas poisoning being talked about on the radio. It was just as well that she couldn't, because what she now saw was so terrifying it made her bury her petrified eyes in her hands.
> A massive cloud of swarming, buzzing, hungry-looking insects was hurtling towards her window. As she watched in terror, the first of the small, black insects crawled through a crack in the window and into the room.

Prompts and Re-creations — Grade E & D Answers

Time for a change of topic and two more <u>E</u> and <u>D grade</u> answers. This will give you an idea of what to <u>include</u> (the good bits) and what to <u>avoid</u> (the not so good bits) in your own writing.

1) For this topic you take a <u>text</u> you know, or you're given a <u>statement</u>, and you have to develop your <u>own</u> piece of <u>creative writing</u> from it.

2) This is your chance to really show off your writing techniques, and to see texts in <u>another way</u>.

Here's a Sample Task and Grade E answer

> Write a creative piece leading up to the final line 'As the oak door slammed and the mirror smashed, laughter could be heard, echoing in her ears.'

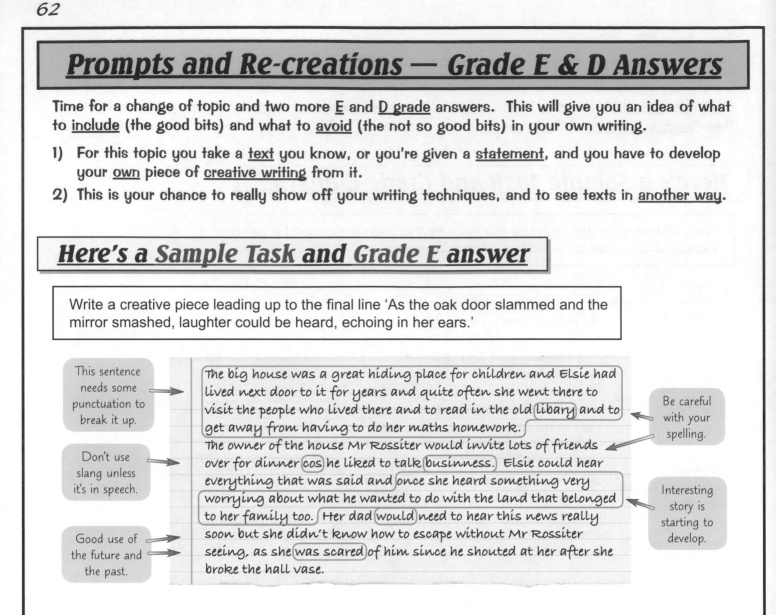

This sentence needs some punctuation to break it up.

Don't use slang unless it's in speech.

Good use of the future and the past.

The big house was a great hiding place for children and Elsie had lived next door to it for years and quite often she went there to visit the people who lived there and to read in the old libary and to get away from having to do her maths homework.
The owner of the house Mr Rossiter would invite lots of friends over for dinner cos he liked to talk businness. Elsie could hear everything that was said and once she heard something very worrying about what he wanted to do with the land that belonged to her family too. Her dad would need to hear this news really soon but she didn't know how to escape without Mr Rossiter seeing, as she was scared of him since he shouted at her after she broke the hall vase.

Be careful with your spelling.

Interesting story is starting to develop.

Here's a Sample Task and Grade D answer

> Write a piece of prose based on a poem in the Relationships cluster of the AQA Anthology.

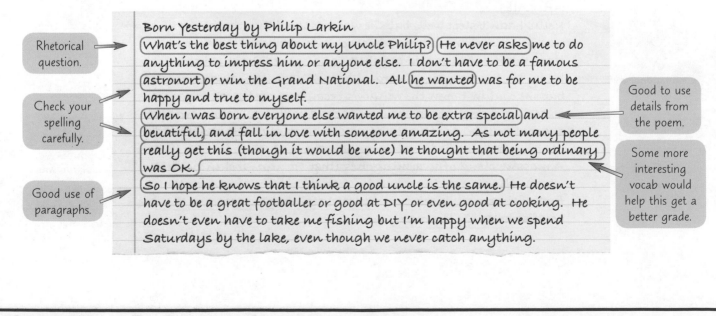

Rhetorical question.

Check your spelling carefully.

Good use of paragraphs.

Born Yesterday by Philip Larkin
What's the best thing about my Uncle Philip? He never asks me to do anything to impress him or anyone else. I don't have to be a famous astronort or win the Grand National. All he wanted was for me to be happy and true to myself.
When I was born everyone else wanted me to be extra special and beuatiful and fall in love with someone amazing. As not many people really get this (though it would be nice) he thought that being ordinary was OK.
So I hope he knows that I think a good uncle is the same. He doesn't have to be a great footballer or good at DIY or even good at cooking. He doesn't even have to take me fishing but I'm happy when we spend Saturdays by the lake, even though we never catch anything.

Good to use details from the poem.

Some more interesting vocab would help this get a better grade.

Prompts and Re-creations — Grade C Answers

Take the same topic, add two fresh <u>tasks</u> and two <u>sample answers</u> and what do you get...
Two <u>C grade</u> answers, fresh from the oven.

Here's a Sample Task and Grade C answer

> Write a creative piece which continues on from the opening line
> 'The town had been deserted for ten long years'.

Be careful with apostrophes.

Good vocabulary.

Nice simile.

Good linking of paragraphs.

The town had been deserted for ten long years. Nobody stirred except the occasional lost bird, looking for food or something to build it's nest. But there were no scraps thrown into the gardens or bins to scavenge, and no field to steal seeds from, because nothing had grown for years. From the faded sign that said 'Welcome to Butterfield', past the deserted supermarket with its grimy window, to the end of the broken railway track, the town was as silent as the grave.

That was until old Jacob rolled into town and parked his rundown trailer. He threw down his tool bag down with a thud and decided that this was going to be his home. "This is where I belong," he said. "Nice quiet place, no folks pokin' their noses into my business".

Good descriptive language.

Good use of speech to develop character.

Here's a Sample Task and Grade C answer

> Write a piece of prose based on a poem in the Relationships cluster of the AQA Anthology.

Good title.

Rhetorical question.

Nice alliteration, but missing apostrophe.

Sister Christina
(Based on 'Sister Maude' by Christina Rossetti')
It was late afternoon and my sister had met her lover behind Father's back again. She had always been his favourite daughter and it was time I showed him that she wasn't acting with the pride and self respect that were so important to him. She needed to be taught a lesson.

How was I to know that it would end in tragedy? I always tried to do the right thing. I did feel bad having to sneak around, watching them from my window acting like they were married. But they weren't married, and their behaviour was wrong!

It was a scorching summers day and the birds chirped merrily as Christina sniffed the scented roses (that I'd grown) then turned to him and laughed.

It wasn't fair. I could never attract someone that special, just because I wasn't born pretty.

Good variety of sentence lengths.

Varied punctuation.

This sentence could do with being broken up a bit more.

Me, Myself, I — Grade E & D Answers

And finally ... here's your third topic and two more tasks and examples of <u>E</u> and <u>D grade</u> answers. Take another look at the mark scheme on p.59 to remind yourself what the marker is looking for.

1) For the <u>Me, Myself, I,</u> topic, you'll be asked to write something from your own <u>personal experience</u>.

2) It's your chance to write about the things that <u>matter to you</u> (e.g. family, school or hobbies).

3) Pick whatever <u>form</u> you think suits what you're writing about, and make a <u>plan</u> before you start.

Here's a Sample Task and Grade E answer

> Write a creative piece with the title 'I wish I'd tried harder'.
> Use whatever form you think is best to produce an effective piece of writing.

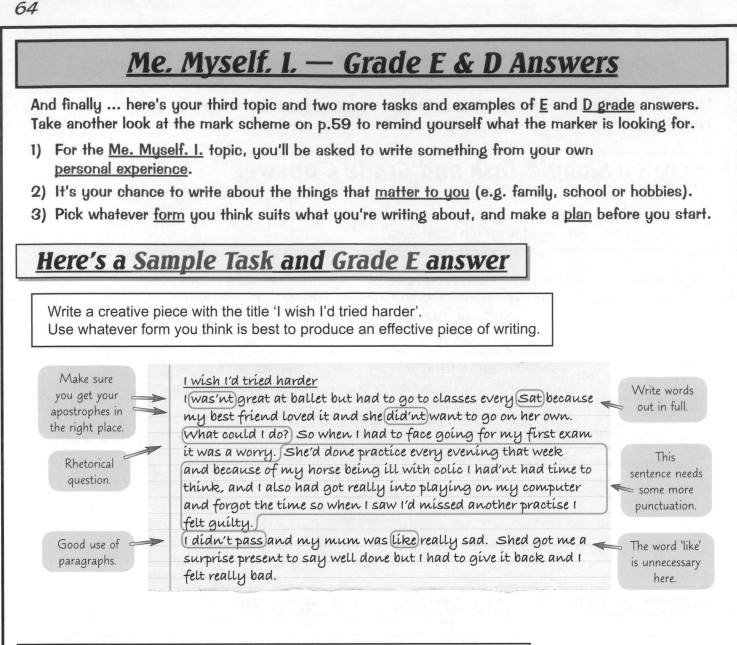

Make sure you get your apostrophes in the right place.

Rhetorical question.

Good use of paragraphs.

Write words out in full.

This sentence needs some more punctuation.

The word 'like' is unnecessary here.

> I wish I'd tried harder
> I was'nt great at ballet but had to go to classes every Sat because my best friend loved it and she did'nt want to go on her own. What could I do? So when I had to face going for my first exam it was a worry. She'd done practice every evening that week and because of my horse being ill with colic I had'nt had time to think, and I also had got really into playing on my computer and forgot the time so when I saw I'd missed another practise I felt guilty.
> I didn't pass and my mum was like really sad. Shed got me a surprise present to say well done but I had to give it back and I felt really bad.

Here's a Sample Task and Grade D answer

> Write about your greatest achievement so far.
> Choose whatever form you think is best to produce an effective piece of writing.

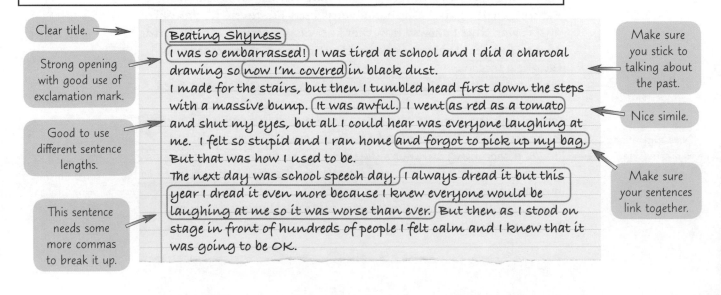

Clear title.

Strong opening with good use of exclamation mark.

Good to use different sentence lengths.

This sentence needs some more commas to break it up.

Make sure you stick to talking about the past.

Nice simile.

Make sure your sentences link together.

> Beating Shyness
> I was so embarrassed! I was tired at school and I did a charcoal drawing so now I'm covered in black dust.
> I made for the stairs, but then I tumbled head first down the steps with a massive bump. It was awful. I went as red as a tomato and shut my eyes, but all I could hear was everyone laughing at me. I felt so stupid and I ran home and forgot to pick up my bag. But that was how I used to be.
> The next day was school speech day. I always dread it but this year I dread it even more because I knew everyone would be laughing at me so it was worse than ever. But then as I stood on stage in front of hundreds of people I felt calm and I knew that it was going to be OK.

Me, Myself, I. — Grade C Answers

It's time to look at two final <u>C grade</u> responses so you can get the hang of all the good things to include in your answers. Then it'll finally be time for a celebratory cuppa and a slice of cake.

Here's a Sample Task and Grade C answer

Write a creative piece with the title 'What really makes me smile'.
Use whatever form you feel is best to produce an effective piece of writing.

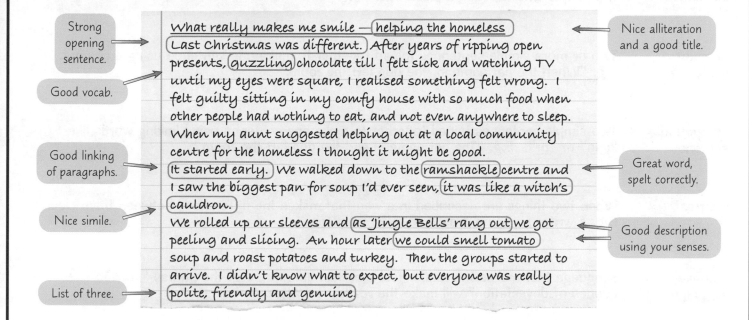

Strong opening sentence.

Good vocab.

Good linking of paragraphs.

Nice simile.

List of three.

What really makes me smile — helping the homeless
Last Christmas was different. After years of ripping open presents, guzzling chocolate till I felt sick and watching TV until my eyes were square, I realised something felt wrong. I felt guilty sitting in my comfy house with so much food when other people had nothing to eat, and not even anywhere to sleep. When my aunt suggested helping out at a local community centre for the homeless I thought it might be good.
It started early. We walked down to the ramshackle centre and I saw the biggest pan for soup I'd ever seen, it was like a witch's cauldron.
We rolled up our sleeves and as 'Jingle Bells' rang out we got peeling and slicing. An hour later we could smell tomato soup and roast potatoes and turkey. Then the groups started to arrive. I didn't know what to expect, but everyone was really polite, friendly and genuine.

Nice alliteration and a good title.

Great word, spelt correctly.

Good description using your senses.

Here's a Sample Task and Grade C answer

Using the form you think is most effective, create a piece of writing called 'They mean the world to me'.

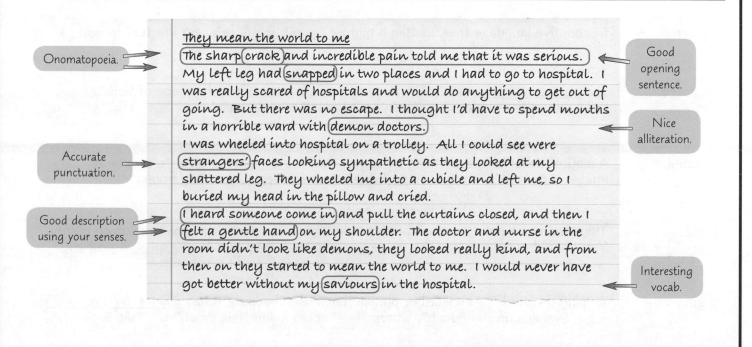

Onomatopoeia.

Accurate punctuation.

Good description using your senses.

They mean the world to me
The sharp crack and incredible pain told me that it was serious.
My left leg had snapped in two places and I had to go to hospital. I was really scared of hospitals and would do anything to get out of going. But there was no escape. I thought I'd have to spend months in a horrible ward with demon doctors.
I was wheeled into hospital on a trolley. All I could see were strangers' faces looking sympathetic as they looked at my shattered leg. They wheeled me into a cubicle and left me, so I buried my head in the pillow and cried.
I heard someone come in and pull the curtains closed, and then I felt a gentle hand on my shoulder. The doctor and nurse in the room didn't look like demons, they looked really kind, and from then on they started to mean the world to me. I would never have got better without my saviours in the hospital.

Good opening sentence.

Nice alliteration.

Interesting vocab.

Glossary

account	A written description of an <u>event</u>.
alliteration	Where the sounds in a phrase are repeated. It's often used to make a phrase stand out. E.g. "the <u>b</u>old, <u>b</u>rash <u>b</u>eat of the <u>b</u>and".
audience	The people who will <u>read</u> a piece of writing.
complex sentence	Two or more simple sentences joined together to make one sentence using a <u>comma</u>. E.g. "When the cat came in, the dog left the room."
compound sentence	Two simple sentences joined together to make one sentence using linking words like "<u>and</u>" or "<u>or</u>". E.g. "The cat came in and the dog left the room."
contrast	When two things are described in a way that makes the <u>differences</u> between them clear. E.g. a writer might contrast two different places.
emotive language	Language that makes the reader feel a certain emotion, e.g. the phrase "horrific scenes of devastation" will make the reader feel angry and disgusted.
exaggeration	Describing something as <u>more</u> or <u>less</u> than it really is, e.g. "a million miles from home".
generalisation	A statement that gives an <u>overall impression</u>, sometimes a misleading one, without going into details. E.g. "Children today eat too much junk food."
imagery	Descriptive language that creates a <u>picture in your mind</u>, bringing the text to life.
language	The <u>choice of words</u> used. The language creates the effect the piece of writing will have on the reader, e.g. it can be informative or persuasive.
metaphor	A way of describing something by saying that it <u>is something else</u>, to create an image in the reader's mind. E.g. "His eyes were deep, black, oily pools."
P.E.E.	This stands for point, example, explanation. This is a technique for developing points. You should make a <u>point</u>, give an <u>example</u> to back it up and then <u>explain</u> it properly.
pun	A "play on words" — a word or phrase that's used because it has <u>more than one meaning</u>. E.g. "She lies on the couch", where "lies" could mean "lies down" or "tells lies".

Glossary

purpose	The <u>reason</u> someone writes a text. E.g. to persuade, to argue, to advise.
quotation	A report of exactly what someone said, which is added to a piece of writing using <u>speech marks</u>. E.g. The prime minister said, "it's not a problem."
repetition	Technique of <u>repeating</u> words or phrases (often three times) for effect.
rhetorical question	A question which <u>doesn't need an answer</u> and tries to persuade the reader to agree with the writer. E.g. "Surely everyone agrees that the future of the planet is important?"
rule of three	Using <u>three</u> describing words together to make an argument or description more effective. E.g. "It was a cold, dark and stormy night."
simile	A way of describing something by <u>comparing</u> it to something else, usually by using the words "like" or "as". E.g. "He was as pale as the moon."
slang	Words or phrases that sound <u>informal</u> e.g. "bloke", "telly".
statistics	<u>Figures</u> from research used to <u>back up</u> points. E.g. "80% of parents agree that school uniform is too expensive."
structure	The <u>order</u> and <u>arrangement</u> of a piece of writing. E.g. how the text begins, develops and ends, whether it uses subheadings or not, etc.
style	The <u>way</u> a text is <u>written</u>, e.g. the type of language and writing techniques used.
subheading	A word or phrase that <u>stands out</u> from the text and <u>divides</u> the text into chunks. It tells you what the <u>next section</u> of text is about.
theme	An <u>idea</u> or <u>topic</u> that's important in a piece of writing. E.g. a story could be based on the theme of forgiveness.
tone	The <u>mood</u> of a piece of writing, e.g. happy, sad, serious, lighthearted. It's an overall effect, created by things like choice of words, imagery and layout.
vocabulary	The range of different <u>words</u> used.

Index